University of Pittsburgh
Pittsburgh, Pennsylvania

Written by Jamie Cruttenden and Tim Williams

Edited by Adam Burns and Meghan Dowdell

Layout by Meryl Sustarsic

Additional contributions by Omid Gohari, Christina Koshzow, Chris Mason, Joey Rahimi, and Luke Skurman

COLLEGE PROWLER®

ISBN # 1-4274-0189-6
ISSN # 1552-1680
© Copyright 2006 College Prowler
All Rights Reserved
Printed in the U.S.A.
www.collegeprowler.com

Last updated 5/16/2006

Special Thanks To: Babs Carryer, Andy Hannah, LaunchCyte, Tim O'Brien, Bob Sehlinger, Thomas Emerson, Andrew Skurman, Barbara Skurman, Bert Mann, Dave Lehman, Daniel Fayock, Chris Babyak, The Donald H. Jones Center for Entrepreneurship, Terry Slease, Jerry McGinnis, Bill Ecenberger, Idie McGinty, Kyle Russell, Jacque Zaremba, Larry Winderbaum, Roland Allen, Jon Reider, Team Evankovich, Lauren Varacalli, Abu Noaman, Mark Exler, Daniel Steinmeyer, Jared Cohon, Gabriela Oates, David Koegler, and Glen Meakem.

Bounce-Back Team: Kevin Nash, Alison Fleming, and Adam Fleming.

College Prowler®
5001 Baum Blvd.
Suite 750
Pittsburgh, PA 15213

Phone: 1-800-229-4675
Fax: 1-800-772-4972
E-Mail: info@collegeprowler.com
Web Site: www.collegeprowler.com

College Prowler® is not sponsored by, affiliated with, or approved by the University of Pittsburgh in any way.

College Prowler® strives faithfully to record its sources. As the reader understands, opinions, impressions, and experiences are necessarily personal and unique. Accordingly, there are, and can be, no guarantees of future satisfaction extended to the reader.

© Copyright 2006 College Prowler. All rights reserved. No part of this work may be reproduced or transmitted in any form or by any means, including but not limited to, photocopy, recording, or any information storage and retrieval systems, without the express written permission of College Prowler®.

Welcome to College Prowler®

During the writing of College Prowler's guidebooks, we felt it was critical that our content was unbiased and unaffiliated with any college or university. We think it's important that our readers get honest information and a realistic impression of the student opinions on any campus—that's why if any aspect of a particular school is terrible, we (unlike a campus brochure) intend to publish it. While we do keep an eye out for the occasional extremist—the cheerleader or the cynic—we take pride in letting the students tell it like it is. We strive to create a book that's as representative as possible of each particular campus. Our books cover both the good and the bad, and whether the survey responses point to recurring trends or a variation in opinion, these sentiments are directly and proportionally expressed through our guides.

College Prowler guidebooks are in the hands of students throughout the entire process of their creation. Because you can't make student-written guides without the students, we have students at each campus who help write, randomly survey their peers, edit, layout, and perform accuracy checks on every book that we publish. From the very beginning, student writers gather the most up-to-date stats, facts, and inside information on their colleges. They fill each section with student quotes and summarize the findings in editorial reviews. In addition, each school receives a collection of letter grades (A through F) that reflect student opinion and help to represent contentment, prominence, or satisfaction for each of our 20 specific categories. Just as in grade school, the higher the mark the more content, more prominent, or more satisfied the students are with the particular category.

Once a book is written, additional students serve as editors and check for accuracy even more extensively. Our bounce-back team—a group of randomly selected students who have no involvement with the project—are asked to read over the material in order to help ensure that the book accurately expresses every aspect of the university and its students. This same process is applied to the 200-plus schools College Prowler currently covers. Each book is the result of endless student contributions, hundreds of pages of research and writing, and countless hours of hard work. All of this has led to the creation of a student information network that stretches across the nation to every school that we cover. It's no easy accomplishment, but it's the reason that our guides are such a great resource.

When reading our books and looking at our grades, keep in mind that every college is different and that the students who make up each school are not uniform—as a result, it is important to assess schools on a case-by-case basis. Because it's impossible to summarize an entire school with a single number or description, each book provides a dialogue, not a decision, that's made up of 20 different topics and hundreds of student quotes. In the end, we hope that this guide will serve as a valuable tool in your college selection process. Enjoy!

OMID GOHARI ◯ CHRISTINA KOSHZOW ◯ CHRIS MASON ◯ JOEY RAHIMI ◯ LUKE SKURMAN ◯
The College Prowler Team

UNIVERSITY OF PITTSBURGH
Table of Contents

By the Numbers............................ **1**

Academics **4**

Local Atmosphere **11**

Safety & Security **18**

Computers.................................. **24**

Facilities...................................... **30**

Campus Dining.......................... **36**

Off-Campus Dining **44**

Campus Housing **55**

Off-Campus Housing................ **64**

Diversity...................................... **69**

Guys & Girls............................... **75**

Athletics...................................... **81**

Nightlife...................................... **89**

Greek Life **99**

Drug Scene.............................. **105**

Campus Strictness **111**

Parking...................................... **116**

Transportation **122**

Weather **129**

Report Card Summary **134**

Overall Experience **135**

The Inside Scoop..................... **139**

Finding a Job or Internship **143**

Alumni **145**

Student Organizations............ **147**

The Best & Worst.................... **152**

Visiting...................................... **154**

Words to Know....................... **158**

Introduction from the Author

I had no idea where to begin looking for the dream university that I had composed in my head. So, blindly, I began the college search. It was fate that led me to the University of Pittsburgh. The glossy pictures in the brochure reflected the closest thing to my dream college that I had seen to date. However, up to a point, the pictures were all I had. Further information and research on the University turned up high academic standards, a large student body with plenty of organizations to get involved in on campus, a bustling city atmosphere with the luxury of not actually being in the city, and more things to do on a Saturday night than you could do in a year.

Yes, everything the brochure and research told me sounded pretty good, and awfully close to this picture-perfect college setting I envisioned. But did I really want to live there for four years? Unfortunately, I had to fly by the seat of my pants, and base my collegiate decision on the brochures. You, however, have a much more powerful resource in your hands. Would I change my decision to go to the University of Pittsburgh if I could have had this book when I was choosing a college? Absolutely not—not in a million years. Hopefully, this book will provide you with enough information for you to make a decision about the University of Pittsburgh, with as much confidence as I have in reflection.

The University of Pittsburgh is climbing up the ladder of recognition every single year. Academic standards have skyrocketed in the last five years. Two of Pitt's varsity sports teams have earned national top 25 rankings. The University offers a variety of majors, as well as graduate school guarantees to those who qualify. A five minute bus ride will get you into the heart of downtown. A five minute bus ride in the other direction will get you so far out of town that you'll think you've left the city. But, all of this does not paint an accurate picture of the University of Pittsburgh. These are the things that I learned from the brochures, and probably what you're trying to dig past by reading this book. Yes, a Pitt degree is becoming an increasingly prestigious thing, and yes, there are plenty of choices in degrees, extracurriculars, and things to do on Saturday night, but college is so much more than classes and parties. College becomes your home for four years, and sometimes longer. Research all that you can, and choose your new home wisely. I hope this book provides you with a more accurate picture of what life is really like at the University of Pittsburgh.

Jamie Cruttenden, Author
University of Pittsburgh

By the Numbers

General Information
University of Pittsburgh
4200 Fifth Ave.
Pittsburgh, PA 15213

Control:
Public

Academic Calendar:
Semester

Religious Affiliation:
None

Founded:
1787

Web Site:
www.pitt.edu

Main Phone:
(412) 624-4141

Admissions Phone:
(412) 624-7488

Student Body
Full-Time Undergraduates:
15,080

Part-Time Undergraduates:
2,101

Total Male Undergraduates:
8,234

Total Female Undergraduates:
8,947

Admissions

Overall Acceptance Rate:
49%

Total Applicants:
18,973

Total Acceptances:
9,295

Freshman Enrollment:
2,991

Yield (% of admitted students who enroll):
32%

Early Decision Available?
No

Early Action Available?
No

Regular Decision Deadline:
Rolling

Must-Reply-By Date:
May 1

Applicants Placed on a Waiting List:
203

Applicants Accepted from Waiting List:
132

Students Enrolled from Waiting List:
82

Transfer Applications Received:
3,252

Transfer Applications Accepted:
892

Transfer Students Enrolled:
637

Transfer Student Acceptance Rate:
27%

Common Application Accepted?
Yes

Supplemental Forms?
No

Admissions Web Site:
www.pitt.edu/admissions.html

SAT I or ACT Required?
Either

First-Year Students Submitting SAT Scores:
99%

SAT I Range (25th–75th Percentile):
1140–1330

SAT I Verbal Range (25th–75th Percentile):
560–650

SAT I Math Range (25th–75th Percentile):
580–670

First-Year Students Submitting ACT Scores:
21%

ACT Composite:
24–28

Retention Rate:
88%

Top 10% of High School Class:
46%

Application Fee:
$35

Financial Information

In-State Tuition:
$11,463

Out-of-State Tuition:
$20,784

Room and Board:
$7,438

Books and Supplies:
$1,000

Average Need-Based Financial Aid Package (including loans, work-study, grants, and other sources):
$10,317

Students Who Applied for Financial Aid:
62%

Students Who Received Aid:
50%

Financial Aid Forms Deadline:
March 1

Financial Aid Phone:
(412) 624-7488

Financial Aid Web Site:
www.pitt.edu/~oafa

Academics

The Lowdown On...
Academics

Degrees Awarded:
Bachelor
Post-Bachelor Certificate
Master
Post-Master Certificate
First-Professional
Doctorate

Most Popular Majors:
15% Business
12% English
12% Social Sciences
10% Engineering
10% Psychology

Undergraduate Schools:
College of Arts and Sciences
College of Business Administration
College of General Studies
School of Health and Rehabilitation Sciences
School of Information Sciences
School of Social Work
Undergraduate School of Engineering
Undergraduate School of Nursing

Full-time Faculty:
1,548

Faculty with Terminal Degree:
92%

Student-to-Faculty Ratio:
15:1

Average Course Load:
15 Credits (5 classes)

Graduation Rates:
Four-Year: 44%
Five-Year: 64%
Six-Year: 67%

Special Degree Options
- The University Honors College (UHC) offers a Bachelor's of Philosophy (BPhil) degree option for undergraduates
- Certificate programs are offered by most schools in a wide variety of areas
- Pre-professional programs: pre-law, pre-med, pre-dentistry, pre-pharmacy
- Five-year programs: Joint degree program; BS Statistics and MA or MS Applied statistics; College of Arts & Sciences (BA or BS) and Engineering (BSE)

Best Places to Study
Cathedral of Learning Commons, Cathedral Lawn, Hillman Library, and residence hall lounges

AP Test Score Requirements
Possible credit and/or placement for scores of 4 or 5

IB Test Score Requirements
Possible credit for scores of 5 to 7

AP Score Credit/Placement
www.advising.pitt.edu/ap/apscores.htm

Sample Academic Clubs
African Students Organization, Blue and Gold Society, Golden Key International Honor Society, Intramural Softball, Model United Nations, Panther Pride Club, Pathfinders, and the Slovak Club

Did You Know?

The University of Pittsburgh's Posvar Hall is built on the site of the old Forbes Field, where the Pirates used to play. **Babe Ruth hit the last two homeruns of his career at that field**, and in commemoration, the home plate is still in the floor of the building. Students slide across home plate for luck, especially during midterms and finals!

Pitt requires you to meet with your **academic advisor at least twice a term** to make sure that you're on top of things.

If you're struggling with classes, Pitt has **multiple tutoring groups, mentoring groups, and a Writing Center** to help you with any problems you may have. Also, at various times throughout the week, TAs set up help desks at tables in the Cathedral, so anyone who has a question or a problem in that particular subject can feel free to walk up and ask!

Students Speak Out On...
Academics

> "The teachers are good—they're the main reason Pitt is ranked highly. All the teachers graduated from places like Cornell, NYU, Harvard, and other crazy schools."

Q "Most of the professors I've had were really cool and helpful, but some weren't. **It's a lot like high school**, but the teachers get paid more."

Q "The quality of the professors sort of depends on which subject you want to major in. Most of them are willing to meet with you if you need help. As long as you show an effort to get in contact with your teachers, they will be helpful. They have office hours when you can visit and ask questions, and they usually give you e-mail addresses and phone numbers to their offices. Even in large classes where you interact more with the teaching assistant, it's still **pretty easy to get in touch with the professor** if you try."

Q "There are **many very good professors**, and then many of them are primarily concerned with their research projects."

Q "I've had good teachers who actually care; I've also had bad ones who couldn't care less, barely spoke English, and were really inexperienced. On the whole, **I think the teachers are pretty average**. In bigger classes, the professors are usually pretty good, and the teaching assistants are really helpful."

Q "**They are pretty good**—the really good ones teach the upper-level courses."

Q "The professors are great. They are really helpful, and all have office hours, which gives **an open door for students** to walk in and ask questions."

Q "The teachers are cool, for the most part. **You can always e-mail them**, and I never felt like there were so many kids that the teacher wasn't willing to help me one-on-one. They're always available, which is great."

Q "All of my teachers have been great, except for one or two. I have larger classes, so it takes more to get to know mine. I make an effort by attending their office hours and e-mailing them. Most of my friends have smaller classes, so they can **meet with their teachers regularly without any hassles**."

Q "Classes are **completely hit or miss**. Sometimes you get an amazing professor who makes you want to come to every single class, and sometimes you get a professor that makes you wish that they didn't require your attendance. But let me tell you, the ones you wish you could take every class with not only outnumber the ones you dislike, but they make the ones you dislike somewhat more bearable."

Q "Generally, I think the professors do a good job of trying to keep the classes interesting and engaging. Some of them are a little bit out there, but **I've never had trouble with a professor** being unhelpful or disagreeable when you try your best."

Q "You can't please everyone all of the time, but I think that most of the professors here are **exactly what you'd find at any other university**."

Q "The teachers vary from department to department, but I've found the professors to be interested in reaching the student body, which sometimes isn't the case in a research school. **Each professor is genuinely concerned** with how much any given student comprehends, and often takes steps out of the classroom if help is requested. The variety of classes offered by the University of Pittsburgh, paired with the integrity of the teachers, is unparalleled to anything that I have seen before."

Q "**A lot of my teachers have taught directly from the book**. Many times I've felt like I could just skip going to class and just read the book, and still be able to keep up with what was going on. As great as that sounds sometimes, I really think that it reflects poorly upon some of the professors at this school."

Q "Some of my classes are huge, and some of my classes are tiny. We are definitely a large university, but in so many ways, I don't feel like the numbers are as high as they are. **You always have access to someone who can help you one-on-one**—either your professor, TA, or a tutor—it's hard to get lost."

The College Prowler Take On...
Academics

The University of Pittsburgh is over 16,000 students strong, which can seem like a scary number, at first. In reality, what you get in classes isn't a reflection of this size. Some classes are large, especially the introductory classes that you have to take for the first year or two, yet once you get heavily focused on your major, the whole university seems to shrink. Variety is the spice of life, and one of the great things about a liberal arts school is that you will find just enough variety to allow you to go in any direction you choose. From a strong medical program based on UMPC's massive resources, to a well-known business program, to a distinguished philosophy department, Pitt has plenty of options for any sort of education you're looking for. Although some programs are stronger than others, and some are smaller (and therefore more personal), Pitt can meet the needs of nearly any student.

Professors and teaching assistants are known for being approachable. The rule at Pitt is that you can find help in any subject—you just have to be willing to go after it. In many cases, you'll find the best professors teaching the highest level courses. Students have complained that some courses, (particularly those in science-related fields), are staffed with foreign teaching assistants that are difficult to understand; while this can sometimes make classes more difficult, there are always other resources available. As the years go by, and the standards for entrance get higher, Pitt is becoming more and more distinguished. The University's strong academic programs are only getting stronger, and students can rest assured that the hard work of earning a degree will pay off.

B

The College Prowler® Grade on
Academics: B

A high Academics grade generally indicates that professors are knowledgeable, accessible, and genuinely interested in their students' welfare. Other determining factors include class size, how well professors communicate, and whether or not classes are engaging.

Local Atmosphere

The Lowdown On...
Local Atmosphere

Region:
Western Pennsylvania

City, State:
Pittsburgh, PA

Setting:
Urban

Distance from Philadelphia:
5 hours

Distance from Cleveland:
2.5 hours

Points of Interest:
Andy Warhol Museum
Benedum Center
Carnegie Museums
Carnegie Science Center
Heinz Fields
Heinz Hall
Kennywood Amusement Park
Pittsburgh Zoo
PNC Park

Closest Shopping Malls or Plazas:

Downtown
Includes Kauffman's, Larrimor's, and Saks Fifth Avenue

The Mall at Robinson
100 Robinson Center Dr.
Robinson
(412) 788-0816
www.shoprobinsonmall.com

Monroeville Mall
200 Monroeville Mall
Monroeville
(412) 243-8511

Pittsburgh Mills
590 Pittsburgh Mills Circle
Tarentum
(724) 904-9000

Ross Park Mall
1000 Ross Park Mall Dr.
Pittsburgh
(412) 369-7493

Southside Works
Outdoor shopping between 26th Street and Hot Metal Street in South Side
Shops include American Eagle Outfitters, Ann Taylor Loft, BCBG Max Azria, Cole Haan, Forever 21, PUMA, Steve Madden, Urban Outfitters, and specialty shops and home stores.

(Shopping, continued)
Shadyside Shops
Including Banana Republic, J.Crew, Victoria's Secret, Gap, Apple Store, and a few specialty shops

The Waterfront
131 East Waterfront Dr.
Homestead
(412) 462-9037

Major Sports Teams:
Pittsburgh Penguins (hockey)
Pittsburgh Pirates (baseball)
Pittsburgh Steelers (football)

Closest Movie Theaters:
Cinemagic Squirrel Hill Theater
5824 Forward Ave.
Squirrel Hill
(412) 421-7900

AMC at the Waterfront
300 W. Waterfront Dr.
Homestead
(412) 462-6384

Manor Cinemagic Theaters
1729 Murray Ave.
Squirrel Hill
(412) 422-7729

City Web Sites:
www.city.pittsburgh.pa.us
www.onlyinoakland.org
www.pittsburgh.com

Did You Know?
5 Fun Facts about Pittsburgh:
- Pittsburgh is the only city whose sports teams all share the same team colors: **black and gold**!
- The Gateway Clipper is **a small fleet of boats that travel the three rivers**, many offering dinner cruises where you can dance the night away.
- The city is home to **the only National Aviary in the country**.
- **Pittsburgh's Schenley Park is one of the largest in-city parks on the East Coast**. It contains plenty of biking and hiking trails, along with an ice rink, swimming pool, and golf course.
- The city boasts **33 colleges and universities**, and sees over 100,000 students return to school each fall.

Local Slang:
Gumband – Rubber band

Pop – What a Pittsburgher calls soda

Red up (redd up) – To clean up

Yinz (yunz) – Rumored to have originated from "you ones;" similar meaning as "y'all"

Famous People from Pittsburgh:

Christina Aguilera	Gene Kelly
George Benson	Henry Mancini
Rachel Carson	Dennis Miller
Perry Como	Fred Rogers
Stephen Foster	Gertrude Stein
Jeff Goldblum	Andy Warhol
Ahmad Jamal	August Wilson
Michael Keaton	

Students Speak Out On...
Local Atmosphere

"The campus is decent because it's spread out in Oakland, which is actually a part of the city of Pittsburgh. There's stuff to do in the Oakland area, such as shop, eat, and go out bar hopping. There are also a few clubs in the area."

"It's a great atmosphere for college students. There are at least five other colleges and universities within a couple of minutes of Pitt. There are places to visit such as downtown, the Incline (Mt. Washington), Station Square, the Strip District, Phipps Conservatory (beautiful flowers and plants), Carnegie Museums (Natural History, Modern Art, and Science Center), the Andy Warhol Museum, PNC Park (home of the Pirates), and Heinz Field (the Steelers and Pitt's own Panthers)—the list goes on and on. I'd be sure to avoid the Hill District and Highland Park. **My basic rule is that if the neighborhood starts with an 'h', I avoid it.**"

"Carnegie Mellon is right next door. It's a huge nerd-growing complex with a skewed guy-to-girl ratio. We all say that at Carnegie Mellon, the odds are good, but the goods are odd. It's all engineering kids who pretty much stick to themselves, though they have nicer frat parties than Pitt. Stay away from the Hill District. It's not too far from campus, but there is nothing of interest there, so you will never have to visit. It's pretty shady. **There are lots of attractions around town**—it's an okay city."

"The atmosphere in Oakland is **very cool and laid-back**. You get to know a lot of people just by walking around the area."

Q "Pittsburgh is a big city, but it's not huge and scary. **Most bands come through here** because we've got a bunch of venues such as the Mellon Arena, Post-Gazette Pavillion, Chevy Amphitheatre, and smaller clubs. There are plenty of places to go, depending on your interests; we have museums, galleries, and an awesome zoo. I grew up here, and I haven't gotten bored of it yet. There are other universities in town, and a bunch of branch campuses."

Q "There are a lot of 'homeless' people in Oakland, many of whom aren't even homeless, but they're all pretty harmless. **Check out the Incline at Mount Washington**, a Panthers football game, and a South Oakland party just for the experience. All in all, it's a great atmosphere to spend your college life in."

Q "I think Pittsburgh is a pretty great town. **It's like a small town with enough people to be a big city**. Each neighborhood has its own character. There are about a dozen other universities in the city, and four in the immediate area."

Q "Stay out of the Hill District and Wilkinsburg late at night if you're alone. Visit Mt. Washington, **all the Carnegie museums, Phipps Conservatory, Schenely Park**, Squirrel Hill, Shadyside, the Waterfront, and downtown."

Q "**Oakland is a wonderful place to study**, with five colleges in the immediate area. There are also ample opportunities to broaden your horizons outside of the classroom, from the Carnegie museums across the street, to the concert venues on Forbes, to the symphony downtown. Stuff to stay away from? Personally, I would avoid the the Original Hot Dog Shop, the 'O,' but that's just because I don't like eating a bucket of grease for lunch."

Q "There is so much to do in this city, and all you have to do is travel a few miles to get out of the city. If you need trees and bike trails and grass, Schenley Park is almost directly across the street from the library. There are **plenty of places to shop**, and there are movie theaters everywhere. If you're really into more cultural sorts of things, there are a number of things to see—the Pittsburgh Symphony, ballets, and plays!"

Q "You could never get bored in this city. **There are always a million and one things to do**! With Duquesne and Carnegie Mellon on either side of Pitt, there are plenty of other campuses to interact with. However, sometimes it's a little overwhelming to try and fit in all the things you want to do!"

Q "There really isn't much interaction between Pitt and the surrounding campuses. I would say if any mixing occurs, it's with Carnegie Mellon. A lot of girls I know go over there for frat parties because they're nicer than the ones at Pitt, and they say the guys over there are nicer. **We don't really see many kids from Duquesne, Carlow, or Chatham.**"

Q "The city is great. It's small and easy to navigate. Not only do you have downtown, and the many cultural experiences it provides, but if you head toward the suburbs, there is even more to be found—especially in the way of shopping! There is never a loss for something to do in this city, which is why **when many people graduate, they don't ever leave.**"

Q "The worst thing about this city is the rough areas. If you make one wrong turn, or get lost driving somewhere, **chances are you'll end up in a not-so-nice area**. Don't get me wrong, most of the time nothing will happen to you if you stumble across these areas; however, they can make you very uncomfortable until you find your way out."

The College Prowler Take On...
Local Atmosphere

Students love the busy city life of Pittsburgh, without the stress of being overwhelmed by an area too large to explore. There are so many different things to do, with different colleges to interact with, that most students have no complaints about the atmosphere in and around campus. In the Oakland area alone, there is enough to do that you can have fun and stay in easy walking distance of Pitt; exploring other neighborhoods, however, expands your experience tenfold.

One of the main complaints about Oakland is the number of beggars. Over time, however, most students figure out that these people are harmless; some would even go as far as to say that the homeless add character to the area. There are a few areas of the city you should stay away from—East Liberty and the Hill District, for example, aren't places you should be if you don't know your way around. The few "bad areas" of the city are mostly out of the way, though, and there's really no reason for students to go there, so you're not likely to stumble into one by accident. Nearly every neighborhood has something to offer, from upscale dining and shopping in Shadyside, to the nightlife in South Side, the cultural districts of Downtown and the North Side, and the restaurants and clubs of Station Square or the Homestead Waterfront. Top that off with three sports teams, the extensive Carnegie library and museums, and a wealth of other attractions, and you have a well-rounded city atmosphere to enhance your college years.

B+

The College Prowler® Grade on Local Atmosphere: B+

A high Local Atmosphere grade indicates that the area surrounding campus is safe and scenic. Other factors include nearby attractions, proximity to other schools, and the town's attitude toward students.

Safety & Security

The Lowdown On...
Safety & Security

Number of Pitt Police:
74 commissioned officers
44 security guards

Pitt Police Department:
Police Department
G1N30 Wesley Posvar Hall
(412) 624-2121 or 811 on campus

Safety Services:
Blue-light phones
Campus shuttles
Crime notices
Crime watch programs
Defense classes
Engraving
Rape aggression defense (RAD)
Residence hall security
Safety seminars
Van call (Saferider)

Health Center Office:

Student Health Service
Medical Arts Building,
Suite 500
3708 Fifth Avenue

For appointments, call
(412) 383-1800

Hours: Monday–Friday
8:30 a.m.–7 p.m.,
Saturday 10 a.m.–3 p.m.,
(on a walk-in basis only)

Health Services:

Basic medical services

Counseling and psychological services

Dermatology

Discounted pharmacy

Gynecology

Health education program

Did You Know?

The University of Pittsburgh has the **third largest police force in Allegheny County**, with 74 police officers who are commissioned and certified in the same way as city or municipal police.

Students Speak Out On...
Safety & Security

> "**The security is great. You have to swipe your student ID to get into different areas of the dormitories, so you don't have to worry about security at all.**"

Q "Pitt has its own police force—not just campus security officers, but actual police officers. They are everywhere, and there are posts with free campus phones and emergency buttons on campus. **I wouldn't walk the streets at night alone**, but that kind of goes without saying."

Q "Pitt probably has **some of the best security you will find**. Every student has an ID card needed to access the residence halls, and there is a guard in a booth at the door of each residence hall. You have to swipe your student ID, and if it registers that you live in that building, the guard lets you enter the building. Guests must be signed into a building by a resident, and the resident is responsible for those guests."

Q "It's pretty good. There are campus cops, sign-ins with ID at all the dorms, and other stuff like that. It is still part of a city at night, but **I'm a chick, and I haven't seen any big problems**."

Q "Of course, **you hear about break-ins or whatever**, but as long as you don't run around dark alleys by yourself, or ignore common sense, you're fine."

Q "The campus security is very, very good. You wouldn't think it would be so good in a city, but it is. **Security within the dorms is intense**."

Q "**I think safety and security here is very good**. Pitt has some of the lowest numbers of thefts, rapes, and other disturbances on campus of any city school. The biggest problem that we have is underage drinking."

Q "The campus is pretty secure. I never walk by myself late at night, but you wouldn't do that anywhere if you wanted to be safe. There are campus shuttles, and **a van you can call at night to pick you up**, and it drive you places. I never have a problem."

Q "People think that going to an urban school immediately means dangerous situations. I beg to differ. I have a lot of friends that go to smaller schools in more rural areas where the streets are darker and emptier. There is less hustle and bustle at these smaller schools, and many more hiding places. Walking home from a party is a scary thing at their schools. On the contrary, **Pitt's campus is well lit**, and there are always people on the streets—all the drunk partiers find their way home by the light of the Cathedral of Learning. I feel much safer on an urban campus than a rural one."

Q "There have been a few assaults in years past, but Pitt has responded well to criticism, and seems to be working hard to make security even better. **Be careful, and walk with friends**—I've never had any real problems, even when running before dawn."

Q "There might be **some small instances of petty theft** on campus, but generally, I feel really safe at Pitt. I don't mind being out alone late at night."

Q "Sometimes it feels like the security to get into dorm rooms is a little over the top, but it is in our best interests. **The Pitt police are definitely a presence on campus**, but they're not too overbearing."

Q "Pitt has its own police force, which is essentially one step down from the city police. There are small Pitt Police stations located in or around most of the dorms, though these often look empty. Between the University's police and local police, however, the entire Oakland campus is covered by police cars—this is especially true at night. **It's rare to hear about crime or safety problems** on or around campus, and Oakland itself generally feels pretty secure."

Q "**Dorm security is ridiculous**. But at least you know that no one is in your building that doesn't belong there."

Q "**There are officers around campus all the time**—on bikes, on foot, in their cruisers. After 10 p.m., there is an officer in the Cathedral of Learning making sure that there isn't anyone in there who doesn't belong. There are always officers making rounds at the library. I think it's nice to actually see them out on campus and know that you're being taken care of."

The College Prowler Take On...
Safety & Security

Common sense is the keyword when you're talking about urban campus security. Many students feel that, as long as you're not asking for trouble, you won't have any problems at Pitt. The campus is always well lit—the University recently invested nearly a million dollars into lighting—and because of the urban location, there are people out on the streets at every hour. Oakland is regularly patrolled by both city and University police, and calls are responded to quickly; this is especially true at night and on the weekends. Dorm security is especially tight; residence halls are guarded 24 hours a day, seven days a week. You can't get into any dorm unless you live there (or are signed in by a resident), and all residents have to swipe their student IDs before entering.

Break-ins and petty thefts tend to be the biggest security issue at Pitt. Both in campus buildings and nearby apartment thefts aren't uncommon. It's best not to leave your stuff unattended, and always remember to lock your doors. The South Oakland area, where many students live when they move off campus, isn't known as the best location; even here, though, the police presence tends to deter any serious crime. Other nearby neighborhoods pose little threat, with the possible exception of the Hill District (which begins at the northern end of campus)—you won't have any reason to go there, anyway. Overall, students feel the same security at Pitt that most only find in smaller, rural schools; as long as you're careful, it's easy to spend four years in Oakland and not have any problems.

B

The College Prowler® Grade on Safety & Security: B

A high grade in Safety & Security means that students generally feel safe, campus police are visible, blue-light phones and escort services are readily available, and safety precautions are not overly necessary.

Computers

The Lowdown On...
Computers

High-Speed Network?
Yes

Wireless Network?
Yes

Number of Labs:
7

Number of Computers:
About 700

Operating Systems:
Mac OSX, Red Hat Linux, Sun Solaris, Windows XP

24-Hour Labs
David Lawrence, Benedum Hall (Tuesday–Thursday), and Sutherland Hall (Tuesday–Thursday)

Charge to Print?
None, unless you print over 900 pages per semester

Free Software
Mac OSX, Microsoft FrontPage 2003, Microsoft Office 2003, Microsoft Office X, Microsoft Visual Studio NET, Microsoft Windows XP Professional, Mulberry, Norton Antivirus

Discounted Software
ArcView, Clementine 7.1, EndNote, Mathcad, Mathematica, Minitab, Oracle, SAS Statistical Software, S-Plus, SPSS

Did You Know?

You can check out where the **wireless network is available**, as well as find information about computing labs, e-mail kiosks, student software, and residential networking at *www.technology.pitt.edu/for_students.html*.

The Pitt Technology **Help Desk is available 24 hours a day, 7 days a week** to consult with students, faculty, and staff on computer problems and information services. To contact the help desk, call (412) 624-HELP.

Students Speak Out On...
Computers

> "The network is nice. It's really fast and almost always works. The labs get crowded during busy times of the day, and during finals week, it's impossible to get into one. If you have a computer to bring, bring it."

Q "The computer network system here is great. **Every residence hall room is wired** for high-speed Ethernet connections. There are many computer labs, and the only times they are overcrowded are around midterms and finals. I would recommend bringing your own computer if you have one, just for convenience."

Q "The computer network at Pitt is decent. Most dorms are equipped with built in network connections, so you can surf the Web, check out library books, and research your next semester's classes from the comfort of your room. There are **a lot of labs on campus**, but as finals approach, they get crowded, and sometimes the printer output is backed up for hours."

Q "No matter where you go to school, **you'll probably need your own computer**, if it's possible. You could still probably get by without a personal computer at Pitt. There are tons of labs, and many are open 24 hours a day."

Q "The on-campus connection is a T1—it's awesome. **The whole computer system is great**, and rarely ever has a problem. Pitt has a bunch of computer labs, and keeps adding more. You definitely don't need your own, but I like privacy when I'm on IM and writing papers, so I brought my own."

Popular Places to Chill:
Cathedral lawn
Hillman Library first floor
The Schenley Quad
Towers lobby

What Is There to Do on Campus?

Take in a basketball game or work out at Petersen Events Center; play some basketball, volleyball, or racquetball at Trees Hall; see a play at Stephen Foster Memorial Theatre; throw a Frisbee on the Cathedral lawn; grab a bite to eat at one of the many on-campus eateries; play some pool or Ping-Pong in the Union; take a walk in Schenley Park.

Movie Theater on Campus?

No

Bowling on Campus?

No

Bar on Campus?

No, but there are two bars a few blocks from the Union.

Coffeehouse on Campus?

Yes, the Cathedral Café in the Cathedral of Learning basement, Cup and Chaucer in the Hillman Library, Café Victoria in Victoria Hall, Common Grounds in Litchfield Towers, the Pennsylvania Perk in Pennsylvania Hall, and the Side Bar in the law building all serve Starbucks coffee; Jazzman's Café in Peterson Events Center offers Seattle's Best coffee.

Favorite Things to Do

A student favorite is Friday Night Improv at the Studio Theatre at 11 p.m. every week. There are always movies being shown in the Union—usually twice a week, on Tuesday and Friday. Be sure to see at least one Pitt football game and one Pitt basketball game during your college career, and play intramurals if you're into sports. Also, be sure to check out a play or two at the Stephen Foster Memorial Theatre.

Students Speak Out On...
Facilities

> "Most of the facilities are either new or recently remodeled. We share our stadium with the Steelers and actually played the inaugural game there in 2001. We just built a new all-purpose building with brand new computer labs and new classrooms."

Q "We recently finished a state-of-the-art basketball arena that is one of the best in the country, and the football team plays off campus at Heinz Field (home of the Pittsburgh Steelers). In the same building as the arena, which also hosts major bands and concerts, we have an **amazing new gym with beautiful equipment and great racquetball courts**. The computer labs are very good. The recently renovated William Pitt Union is the student center, and it serves the purpose very well."

Q "The classrooms are nice and pretty new. There are gyms all around campus, but they aren't that great, except for the one at the Peterson Events Center. **The student union has a big pool table room** and assembly rooms where they run new movies for a few dollars several nights a week. It's nice, but you really don't spend too much time in there unless you like to play pool a lot, I guess."

Q "**Athletic facilities are pretty good**—there are two gyms on lower campus, a bigger one on upper campus that the guys usually go to, and a huge newer one. I don't really know too much about the computer labs—they are all over the place, though."

Q "If you can afford to bring your own computer, I definitely would. Too many students around midterms and finals clog up the computer labs, and it's hard to budget your time around that. **Having your own computer is not only a huge convenience, but a time-saver as well**. One thing that is really nice about Pitt is that they make all of the latest software available for students for no extra charge, and plus all of the residence halls are equipped with Ethernet, so it makes for a fast connection."

Q "I didn't have my own computer freshman year, and I managed to get all of my work done in a decent amount of time. David Lawrence is a good place to go if you need a computer late at night, or at the last minute. Tip: **use the top floors in the library for computers**. It seems as if a lot of people don't like Macs, so if you do, there's always a terminal available."

Q "You should bring your own computer, just for personal use. **The only bad lab is in the Cathedral of Learning**—it is always packed from around 12 p.m. to 4 p.m., but there are six other labs I can name off the top of my head that always have an open computer. Most labs have PCs, but some use Macs. I think that Pitt also gives you something like 900 free printing pages a semester, and if you print them front and back, it actually turns out to be 1,800 free pages."

Q "Computer labs are crowded, but you can usually get on one right away or within five to ten minutes. I thought having a computer was helpful, especially in the dorms, because **there are hookups in the rooms**. You definitely don't need one to get by, but it's a nice convenience."

Q "I think everyone needs their own computer. Now, this is not a requirement, and you can use the labs, but it will make your life so much easier. You can get a decent computer for $600 now, so really, you shouldn't have too much trouble if you start saving early! **The labs can be crowded**, but you can get in to do what you need to do."

Q "The computer network is amazingly fast. It rarely goes down. **The computer labs are almost never crowded**, except for peak times during the day, such as around lunch time. Whether to bring a computer or not is up to you, but I know that I keep one just for convenience sake."

Q "The residence hall network is average in and of itself—not great, not awful—but Computing Services offers timely and efficient service and help to students. The computer labs themselves are usually not too busy, and there are **enough labs close to one another to accommodate the overflow**. Having your own computer is convenient, but much less necessary than at other universities."

Q "Don't even think about procrastinating on papers around midterm and finals time, at least if you use the labs. They get crazy! **Everyone fights for computers when it comes down to crunch time**. That's one of the nice things about bringing your own computer—you don't ever have to wait at the lab."

Q "Having your own computer is a must for almost any college, and this is just as true at Pitt. The dorms are equipped with high-speed Internet that has remarkably few problems or network outages. **Bandwidth is definitely not an issue**, and network/technology resources are relatively easy to access. There are quite a few computer labs on campus, so generally, crowding isn't an issue; however, lab computers are notoriously slow and annoying."

Q "Each residence hall has Internet connections in all of their rooms, which is great if you have your own computer. **The connection is lightning fast**, and you definitely get spoiled. When you go home and use your regular Internet connection, you get so mad at it because it goes so much slower than the one you use at Pitt."

The College Prowler Take On...
Computers

Pitt's high-speed network supports all of the connections on campus, which include every residence hall, seven public computing labs, e-mail kiosks scattered across campus, and growing wireless coverage. Students are happy with both the network speed and the university's support resources. There are trained technicians in every computing lab, two of which are open 24 hours a day during the school year; in addition, the Technology Help Desk is continually staffed with technicians to help students work through computer problems. For those who bring their own computers, Pitt's networking assistants can come to your dorm room to directly assist with software troubles.

The University's computing services are expanding every year, and theycontinue to grow visibly. A wireless network is available in the Cathedral of Learning, the Cathedral of Learning lawn, Pitt Union, Posvar Hall, and the Petersen Events Center, which allows students with laptops more freedom to work where they choose (for those who do bring laptops). Despite this growth, however, the facilities still lag somewhat behind student needs—labs can get crowded during the day and around finals, and both lab computers and kiosks are known for being slow. If you're looking for a quiet place to work, be sure to check out the top floors of the Hillman Library, the Sutherland Hall lab, and Alumni Hall—these seem to be the less-crowded areas, though it all depends on when you go. It's also common to find people waiting in line to use lab PCs while Mac terminals are sitting empty, so it would make sense to learn OSX if you're just trying to type a paper or check your e-mail.

B

The College Prowler® Grade on
Computers: B

A high grade in Computers designates that computer labs are available, the computer network is easily accessible, and the campus' computing technology is up-to-date.

Facilities

The Lowdown On...
Facilities

Student Center:
William Pitt Union

Athletic Center:
Peterson Events Center
Trees Hall

Campus Size:
132 acres

Libraries:
Bevier Engineering Library
Business Library
Chemistry Library
Darlington Memorial Library
Dick Thornburgh Collection
Frick Fine Arts Library
GSPIA/Economics Library
Hillman Library
Information Sciences Library
Langley Library
Mathematics Library
Music Library
Physics Library

Popular Places to Chill:
Cathedral lawn
Hillman Library first floor
The Schenley Quad
Towers lobby

What Is There to Do on Campus?
Take in a basketball game or work out at Petersen Events Center; play some basketball, volleyball, or racquetball at Trees Hall; see a play at Stephen Foster Memorial Theatre; throw a Frisbee on the Cathedral lawn; grab a bite to eat at one of the many on-campus eateries; play some pool or Ping-Pong in the Union; take a walk in Schenley Park.

Movie Theater on Campus?
No

Bowling on Campus?
No

Bar on Campus?
No, but there are two bars a few blocks from the Union.

Coffeehouse on Campus?
Yes, the Cathedral Café in the Cathedral of Learning basement, Cup and Chaucer in the Hillman Library, Café Victoria in Victoria Hall, Common Grounds in Litchfield Towers, the Pennsylvania Perk in Pennsylvania Hall, and the Side Bar in the law building all serve Starbucks coffee; Jazzman's Café in Peterson Events Center offers Seattle's Best coffee.

Favorite Things to Do
A student favorite is Friday Night Improv at the Studio Theatre at 11 p.m. every week. There are always movies being shown in the Union—usually twice a week, on Tuesday and Friday. Be sure to see at least one Pitt football game and one Pitt basketball game during your college career, and play intramurals if you're into sports. Also, be sure to check out a play or two at the Stephen Foster Memorial Theatre.

Students Speak Out On...
Facilities

"Most of the facilities are either new or recently remodeled. We share our stadium with the Steelers and actually played the inaugural game there in 2001. We just built a new all-purpose building with brand new computer labs and new classrooms."

Q "We recently finished a state-of-the-art basketball arena that is one of the best in the country, and the football team plays off campus at Heinz Field (home of the Pittsburgh Steelers). In the same building as the arena, which also hosts major bands and concerts, we have an **amazing new gym with beautiful equipment and great racquetball courts**. The computer labs are very good. The recently renovated William Pitt Union is the student center, and it serves the purpose very well."

Q "The classrooms are nice and pretty new. There are gyms all around campus, but they aren't that great, except for the one at the Peterson Events Center. **The student union has a big pool table room** and assembly rooms where they run new movies for a few dollars several nights a week. It's nice, but you really don't spend too much time in there unless you like to play pool a lot, I guess."

Q "**Athletic facilities are pretty good**—there are two gyms on lower campus, a bigger one on upper campus that the guys usually go to, and a huge newer one. I don't really know too much about the computer labs—they are all over the place, though."

Q "The facilities are nice on campus. Pitt is building several new buildings and has recently opened Sennot Square along with the Petersen Events Center. Some buildings are old, such as the Cathedral of Learning—the main building where classes are held but **Pitt is working to modernize the campus**."

Q "They just put in a new sports complex. There are lots of computer labs, and **the student center is pretty cool**, too. It has pool tables, TVs, and large lounges; though, since we're right in the city, most people find other places to do stuff."

Q "Everything is up to today's standards of being technologically advanced. **The dorms have fitness centers and Internet connections** for every room. The William Pitt Union is the center of student interaction."

Q "The facilities are all pretty good. **Some gyms need renovation**, but most are adequate or very good. I never have problems. The computer labs are state-of-the-art, and the student center is nice, with plenty of room to sit and hang out."

Q "Everything's really **nice and convenient**. Pitt's a large school with a large campus, but things are built right up on campus, and not spread throughout the city, so walking isn't so bad."

Q "The Peterson Events Center is a huge building that looks like some sort of arena in Boston or DC. The basketball team plays there, and May graduation also take place there. There are also **eating and shopping places**, another weight room, and all kinds of student facilities inside. I love it, even though it's a bit of a hike up the hill!"

Q "The buildings are nice, and easy to get to. The campus is filled with grass and trees, so if you are not used to the city, it's not overwhelming. As far as the inside of the buildings goes, some classrooms are great, while others have uncomfortable chairs. The **Cathedral is slowly getting air conditioned**, which can be pretty painful for summer classes."

Q "I think most of the facilities on campus are really nice. Things are generally pretty clean and well lit. Some centers could use more of their respective equipment, but **I've never felt as if something was crappy**."

Q "The Peterson Events Center is gorgeous. The student center is a dressed down hotel, so there are still pieces of flair to it, but they have dressed it down enough so it feels okay to visit it in your pajamas. **The computer labs are always being updated**, although I wish they would replace some of the chairs."

Q "**Our athletic facilities are gorgeous**. The Peterson Events Center gym is hooked up, not to mention they put some great new eateries in there that work with the meal plan. Trees Hall got some more equipment, although some areas of that facility could use some reworking."

Q "The libraries are great for all of your studying needs, and I think **students here don't utilize the Union enough**. Most people go to the Union to buy tickets or to eat, but there is a whole study area along with a great game room that most students never even use. Many of the pool and Ping-Pong tables go untouched for hours at a time, which I really feel is a shame."

The College Prowler Take On...
Facilities

If you're looking for first-rate athletic facilities, you won't be disappointed by what Pitt has to offer. The Petersen Events Center, a new state-of-the-art basketball and recreation arena, boasts a couple rows of cardiovascular machines and a large free-weight area, as well as new eateries that work on Pitt's meal plan. This is also where freshman convocation, graduation, and many on-campus ceremonies, concerts, and performances are now held. "The Pete" supplements a number of older athletic facilities, which include pools, track areas, and other indoor practice and weight rooms. The main residence halls also have smaller gyms attached; though, the equipment in these is noticeably older.

The Hillman Library, the University's primary collection, has four floors and enough volumes to make research really convenient. If you need something else, you can also access smaller, subject-oriented libraries that are located across campus. Pittsburgh's Carnegie Library is available to students as well and is located less than a block from Hillman. The William Pitt Union, a recently-renovated student center, offers a food court and plenty of activities; unlike many other schools, however, the Union has not become a hub of student life. For starters, it's not overly large—besides the game room and eateries, much of the building contains offices. The food court doesn't offer much in the way of selection, but is still a favorite over the weekends for its Freshens Yogurt stand and fast food.

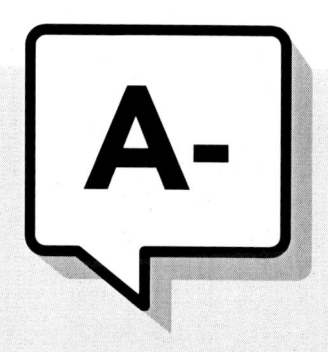

A-

The College Prowler® Grade on Facilities: A-

A high Facilities grade indicates that the campus is aesthetically pleasing and well-maintained; facilities are state-of-the-art, and libraries are exceptional. Other determining factors include the quality of both athletic and student centers and an abundance of things to do on campus.

Campus Dining

The Lowdown On... Campus Dining

Freshman Meal Plan Requirement?
Yes

Meal Plan Average Cost:
$1,320 per semester

Places to Grab a Bite with Your Meal Plan:

Café a la Cart
Location: Langley Hall
Food: Breakfast snacks, deli sandwiches, coffee, drinks
Hours: Monday–Friday 7:30 a.m.–2:30 p.m.

The Cathedral Café
Food: International, soups sandwiches, Chick-fil-A
Location: Cathedral of Learning, ground floor
Hours: Monday–Thursday 10:30 a.m.–6 p.m.,
Friday 10:30 a.m.–5 p.m.,

Eddie's Café
Food: American, Mexican, fast food, salad bar
Location: Litchfield Towers, lower level
Hours: Monday–Friday 11 a.m.– 8 p.m.,
Sunday 11 a.m.–11 p.m.,
(limited eating after 8 p.m.)

Einstein's Express
Food: Bagels, pastries, coffee
Location: Benedum Hall
Hours: Monday–Thursday 7:30 a.m.–7 p.m.,
Friday 7:30 a.m.–3 p.m.

Einstein's On the Way
Food: Bagels, sandwiches, soups, sandwiches, coffee
Location: Posvar Hall, second floor
Hours: Monday–Thursday 7:30 a.m.–7 p.m.,
Friday 7:30 a.m.–3 p.m.

The Marketplace
Food: All-you-can-eat American dining
Location: Litchfield Towers, lower level

(The Marketplace, continued)
Hours: Monday–Thursday 7 a.m.–7 p.m.,
Friday 10:30 a.m.–1:30 p.m.,
Saturday–Sunday 10 a.m.–2 p.m.

Petersen Events Center Food Court
Food: BBQ Blues, Burger King, Sky Ranch Grill, La Vincita, Subversions, Jazzman's Cafe
Location: Petersen Events Center Concourse
Alamo Ranchero Hours: Monday–Friday 10:30 a.m.–7 p.m.,
Burger King Hours: Monday–Friday 7 a.m.–7 p.m., Saturday–Sunday 11 a.m.–6 p.m.,
Jazzman's Cafe Hours: Monday–Friday 7 a.m.–10 p.m., Saturday–Sunday 11 a.m.–9 p.m.
La Vincita Hours: Monday–Friday 10:30 a.m.–7 p.m., Saturday–Sunday 11 a.m.–6 p.m.,
Subversions Hours: Monday–Friday 10:30 a.m.–7 p.m., Saturday–Sunday 11 a.m.–6 p.m.

Schenley Café
Food: Pizza Hut, Orville & Wilbur's, Freshens Yogurt, Sub Connection
Location: William Pitt Union
Hours: Monday–Thursday 7:30 a.m.–12 a.m.,
Friday 7:30 a.m.–9 p.m.,
Saturday 11 a.m.–10 p.m.,
Sunday 4 p.m.–10 p.m.

Sutherland Dining
Food: All-you-can-eat American
Location: Sutherland Hall
Hours: Monday–Thursday 7:30 a.m.–11 a.m., Friday 7:30 a.m.–10 p.m. (limited menu from 2 p.m.–10 p.m.), Saturday 10 a.m.–10 p.m. (limited menu from 2 p.m.–10 p.m.), Sunday 10 a.m.–7 p.m.

Sutherland Snack Shop
Food: Take-out, fast food
Location: Sutherland Hall
Hours: Monday–Thursday 7:30 a.m.–11 p.m., Friday 7:30 a.m.–10 p.m., Saturday 10 a.m.–10 p.m., Sunday 10 a.m.–7 p.m.

Coffee Carts on Campus:

Café Victoria
Location: 3500 Victoria Street, Victoria Hall
Hours: Monday–Thursday 7:30 a.m.–2 p.m.

Cathedral Coffee
Location: Cathedral of Learning, ground floor
Hours: Monday–Thursday 7 a.m.–8 p.m., Friday 7 a.m.–4 p.m.

Common Grounds
Location: Litchfield Towers, lobby
Hours: Monday–Thursday 7:30 a.m.–10 p.m., Friday 7 a.m.–2 p.m., Sunday 4 p.m.–10 p.m.

Cup & Chaucer
Location: Hillman Library
Hours: Monday–Thursday 8:30 a.m.–10 p.m., Friday 8:30 a.m.–4 p.m., Saturday 12 p.m.–5 p.m., Sunday 12 p.m.–10 p.m.

The Pennsylvania Perk
Location: Pennsylvania Hall
Hours: Monday–Thursday 7:30 a.m.–10 p.m., Friday 7:30 a.m.–2 p.m., Sunday 4 p.m.–10 p.m.

The Side Bar
Location: School of Law
Hours: Monday–Friday 7:30 a.m.–2 p.m.

24-Hour On-Campus Eating?
No

Student Favorites:
Eddie's Café
Schenley Café

Other Options

Many students like to treat themselves to lunch or dinner at many of the restaurants within a few blocks walking distance. Although the actual University of Pittsburgh meal plan doesn't work off campus, students have the option of placing Panther Funds on their student ID; these are accepted at many area eating establishments. Student favorites include Hemingway's Café, Subway, the Original Hot Dog Shop, and Dave and Andy's Ice Cream. Check out the Web site *www.pc.pitt.edu/card/merchants.html* for a full list of merchants.

Did You Know?

Schenley Plaza, the park across from Hillman Library, opening soon, has several **food kiosks featuring local and ethnic favorites** with never-ending lines of famished Pitt students, regardless of the weather conditions. On sunny days, the recently built park provides a place for students to relax and nosh on their quick eats, or even to take a ride on the park's working carousel.

Students Speak Out On...
Campus Dining

> "The food on campus is pretty good, for the most part. There are two all-you-can-eat cafeterias, and other places like Pizza Hut and sub shops. I recommend the Marketplace and Sub Connection."

Q "The food is pretty good. I am just warning you that wherever you go, you will get sick of it after a while. We have a lot of food choices, including Pizza Hut, a sub place, hamburgers, tacos, salad bars, and hot meals. There are buffet-style dining halls where you can eat as much as you want, as well as á la carte places where you can get single dishes, or **stock up on cereal, milk, fruit, and chips for your dorm**. All of these places take the school's meal plan and are excellent for using up money that you'd lose otherwise. I don't really know of one good place; they're all good. It depends on what you like the most."

Q "The Pitt dining plan is one of the main reasons I'll be moving off campus after this semester. Although every café presents a different image, **there's really very little variety in the food**. Many of the eateries are essentially fast food; not only is this unhealthy, but it gets old really quickly. The University claims to provide vegetarian and vegan meals, but these tend to be low-quality and hard to find. The meal plan itself entails buying "meal blocks"—based on the plan you choose, you get a certain number each week. Once the week is over, any unused meal blocks disappear. Now that I know how terrible campus dining is, I really regret not getting the smallest meal plan and using the rest of my food money to eat off campus."

Q "I never ate on campus at Pitt. **You can put money on your Pitt ID card** and use it at some off campus restaurants and fast food places, so you don't have to eat on campus all the time. If you live on campus, though, there's no way around it."

Q "Some of the major dining halls have places you've actually heard of before: Chick-fil-A, Pizza Hut. The Marketplace, or whatever they're calling it now, is a buffet-style place that **seemed to have gotten worse as the years went on**, but the food is edible, and there is enough variety to find something you like. They also offer vegetarian, vegan, and different religious meals."

Q "The food is okay. It's a lot better then some schools I have been to, but like anything, it gets old. **There are fast food places all around** the campus."

Q "If you're diet conscious, C-Side, now the Marketplace, is the best place to eat because you have more options. It's also the best for any meal plan because it's buffet style. Eddie's, under Tower A, is probably the second best in terms of variety, but **the most popular place to eat is Schenley in the Union.**"

Q "There are two all-you-can-eat places, and the Union has a Pizza Hut and a sub place. There's also a Chick-fil-A and cafeteria in the Cathedral. All in all, the food is pretty good, but **everyone is just sick of it by the end of the year**."

Q "**The food is excellent**. Almost every dining hall is equipped with a Starbucks, and we also have a Pizza Hut. C-Side has an all-you-can-eat buffet, and there are many other places on campus."

Q "Eating on campus is okay. I recommend using your Pitt funds on restaurants off campus, because **the stuff on campus can get old** really quickly."

Q "I haven't eaten food on campus in a while, but it was pretty good, with lots of choices. There's a cafeteria and a couple other places with lots of stuff. They also added a sub shop. **The Cathedral is the best place to use food blocks**; it has sushi, good sandwiches and salads, and a Chick-fil-A."

Q "The food is really good—a lot of my friends who visit from other schools are surprised at how good it is. There are only about five or six cafeterias on campus, but they're **located just where you need them, and all have a huge selection**."

Q "The key word is variety. There is everything from vegetarian to international cuisine on campus. There are also many chain restaurants. The **beauty of the Pitt meal plan is that you can change it whenever** you want during the year, so you don't lose your money."

Q "Dining halls aren't bad at all. **You'll get bored with the food eventually**, but that's the same on every campus in the United States. Try the Cathedral Café and the food at the Petersen Events Center for a real treat!"

Q "The food is good, comparatively. The Cathedral Café is the favorite of many, boasting a Chick-fil-A and a tasty sandwich shop. Each dining hall has its own hot spot, or favorite place among the students. **The sub place at Schenley Café is great**, and Eddie's is the best place to burn off your meal blocks at the end of the week."

The College Prowler Take On...
Campus Dining

All students living in residence halls are required to get a meal plan. Each of the six plans varies in the amount of meal blocks (dining units equivalent to about $5.25) and Dining Dollars (food-only money that supplements meal blocks), and are accessible through your student ID at dining halls and food carts. You get more meal blocks with every plan, but these come allotted into a certain number each week; unused meal blocks expire at the end of the day on Sunday. Dining Dollars last the entire semester, but they are only supplementary—you get about $200 per semester, depending on the plan. Weekends see students scrambling to use up extra blocks.

There are a number of eateries located across Pitt's campus, each set in a different style. Eddie's and the Schenley Café are the busiest. Both are food-court style, and have a number of different features. The all-you-can-eat cafeterias boast more variety than any other eateries, though students say that the food still gets old quickly. Overall, many students are satisfied with the quality and availability of Pitt's dining services. However, meal plans can get costly—if you don't use up all your meal blocks each week, you'll lose them—and there's not a great deal of variety across the dining halls. Also, between the sporadic hours and lack of 24-hour eating, you'll find yourself in Oakland's local restaurants on many nights and weekends. This would be fine if the meal plan worked there, but unfortunately no restaurants off-campus take meal blocks or Dining Dollars, only Panther Funds, the declining debit account each student can activate on their ID cards.

B-

The College Prowler® Grade on Campus Dining: B-

Our grade on Campus Dining addresses the quality of both school-owned dining halls and independent on-campus restaurants as well as the price, availability, and variety of food.

Off-Campus Dining

The Lowdown On...
Off-Campus Dining

Restaurant Prowler: Popular Places to Eat!

Buffalo Blues
Food: American/BBQ
216 S. Highland Ave., Shadyside
(412) 362-5837
Cool Features: TVs everywhere, great for watching sports.
Price: $6–$12 per person
Hours: Monday–Friday 11 a.m.–11 p.m., Saturday–Sunday 12 p.m.–12 a.m., Bar open until 2 a.m.

Casbah
Food: Mediterranean and North African
229 S. Highland Ave., Shadyside
(412) 661-5656
www.bigburrito.com/casbah
Cool Features: Unique, ever-evolving menu.
Price: $20–$25 per person
Hours: Monday–Thursday 11:30 a.m.–2:30 p.m. and 5 p.m.–10 p.m.,
Friday 11:30 a.m.–2:30 p.m., and 5 p.m.–11 p.m.,
Saturday 5 p.m.–11 p.m.,
Sunday 11 a.m.–2 p.m. and 5 p.m.–9 p.m.

China Palace

Food: Chinese

5440 Walnut St., Shadyside

(412) 687-RICE

*http://chinapalace
pittsburgh.com*

Price: $6–$18 per person

Cool Features: Discounted lunch specials.

Hours: Monday–Thursday 11:30 a.m.–10 p.m., Friday–Saturday 11:30 a.m.–11 p.m., Sunday 2 p.m.–9 p.m.

Cozumel

Food: Mexican

5505 Walnut St., Shadyside

(412) 621-5100

Price: $5–$15 per person

Cool Features: Discounted lunch and drink specials throughout the week.

Hours: Monday–Friday 11 a.m.–2:30 p.m., 5 p.m.–10 p.m., Saturday 12 p.m.–10 p.m., Sunday 12 p.m.–9 p.m.

Craig Street Coffee

Food: Sandwiches, salads

305 S. Craig St., Oakland

(412) 683-9993

*http://web.craigstreet
coffee.com*

Cool Features: Vegetarian options, close to campus.

Price: $3–$13 per person

Hours: Monday–Friday 7:30 a.m.–6 p.m., Saturday 8 a.m.–5:30 p.m.

Dave & Andy's Homemade Ice Cream

207 Atwood St., Oakland

(412) 681-9906

Cool Features: Incredible variety of ice cream, including birthday cake with real cake, and bubble gum. Waffle cones are also home-made and made by waffle iron.

Price: $4–$6 per person

Hours: Monday–Friday 11:30 a.m.–10 p.m., Saturday–Sunday 12 p.m.–10 p.m.

Eat 'n Park

Food: Diner fare

1816 Murray Ave., Squirrel Hill

(412) 422-7203

www.eatnpark.com

Cool Features: Smiley face cookies, open late, and serves a good breakfast buffet.

Price: $5–$8 per person

Hours: Daily 24 hours

Fuel & Fuddle

Food: American

212 Oakland Ave., Oakland

(412) 682-3473

www.fuelandfuddle.com

Cool Features: Features a half-price menu after 11 p.m., as well as one of the largest import beer selections in Oakland.

Price: $6–$16 per person

Hours: Daily 11 a.m.–2 a.m.

Hard Rock Café
Food: American
230 W. Station Square Dr., Station Square
(412) 481-7625
www.hardrock.com
Cool Features: Bands come often, some tickets sold in advance through Ticketmaster.
Prices: $8–$15 per person
Hours: Sunday–Thursday
11 a.m.–11 p.m.
Bar open until 12 a.m.,
Friday–Saturday
11 a.m.–12 a.m.
Bar open until 2 a.m.

Hemingway's Café
Food: American
3911 Forbes Ave., Oakland
(412) 621-4100
Cool Features: Features a half-price menu every day after 9 p.m., as well as daily all-day $1 beer specials for the over-21 crowd.
Price: $6–$10 per person
Hours: Monday–Saturday
11 a.m.–2 a.m.,
Sunday 6 p.m.–2 a.m.

India Garden
Food: Indian
328 Atwood St., Oakland
(412) 682-3000
Cool Features: Half-price menu from 4 p.m.–6 p.m., and 10 p.m.–1 a.m.
Price: $8–$16 per person
Hours: Daily 11 a.m.–1 a.m.

Joe Mama's Italian Delux
Food: Italian
3716 Forbes Ave., Oakland
(412) 621-7282
Cool Features: Half-price pasta menu after 11 p.m.
Price: $6–$15 per person
Hours: Daily 11 a.m.–2 a.m.

Lucca
Food: Northern Italian, fine dining
317 S. Craig St., Oakland
(412) 682-3310
Cool Features: Outdoor dining.
Price: $10–$25 per person
Hours: Monday–Thursday
11:30 a.m.–2:30 p.m. and 5:30 p.m.–10 p.m.,
Friday 11:30 a.m.–2:30 p.m. and 5:30 p.m.–11:30 p.m.,
Saturday 5:30 p.m.–11 p.m.,
Sunday 4:30 p.m.–9 p.m.

LuLu's Noodle Shop and Yum Wok
Food: Asian
400 S. Craig St., Oakland
(412) 681-3333
Cool Features: Bubble drinks, as well as large and small menu items.
Price: $10–$15 per person
Hours: Daily 11 a.m.–9:20 p.m.

Mad Mex
Food: Mexican
370 Atwood St., Oakland
(412) 681-5656
Cool Features: Happy Hour—
$6 20 oz. margaritas from
4 p.m.–6 p.m., and 9 p.m.–
11 p.m., and half-priced menu
after 11 p.m.
Price: $10–$15 per person
Hours: Daily 11 a.m.–1 a.m.,
Bar open until 2 p.m.

Max and Erma's
Food: American
5533 Walnut St., Shadyside
(412) 681-5775
Cool Features: Sundae bar.
Price: $8–$15 per person
Hours: Sunday–Thursday
11:30 a.m.–10 p.m., Saturday–
Sunday 11:30 a.m.–11 p.m.

The Original Hot Dog Shop (The O)
Food: American, fast food
3901 Forbes Ave., Oakland
(412) 621-7388
Cool Features: Pitt staple,
known for its massive cheese
fries, greasy pizza, and dirt-
cheap prices.
Price: $2–$8 per person
Hours: Daily 10 a.m.–5 a.m.

Pamela's
Food: American, breakfast
3703 Forbes Ave., Oakland
(412) 683-4066
or
5527 Walnut St., Shadyside
(412) 683-1003
or
5813 Forbes Ave., Squirrel Hill
(412) 422-9457
Cool Features: Award-winning
greasy breakfasts.
Price: $7–$10 per person
Hours: Oakland, daily,
7:30 a.m.–4 a.m.; Shadyside
and Squirrel Hill, Monday–
Saturday 8 a.m.–4 p.m.,
Sunday 9 a.m.–3 p.m

Panera Bread
Food: Sandwiches,
salads, soups
3800 Forbes Ave., Oakland
412-683-3727
www.panerabread.com
Cool Features: Constant supply
of bread and pastry samples
perfect for starving college
kids low on cash.
Hours: Monday–Friday
6 a.m.–9 p.m.,
Saturday 7 a.m.–9 p.m.,
Sunday 8 a.m.–8 p.m.

Pittsburgh Deli Company
Food: Sandwiches,
soups, salads
728 Copeland St., Shadyside
(412) 682-3354

(Pittsburgh Deli Company, continued)
www.pghdeli.com
Cool Features: Hosts live music from local bands.
Price: $6–$10 per person
Hours: Daily 11 a.m.–12 a.m., Bar open until 2 a.m.

Primanti Brothers
Food: American, fast food
3803 Forbes Ave., Oakland
(412) 621-4444
www.primantibros.com
Cool Features: Food served late.
Price: $5–$10 per person
Hours: Sunday–Wednesday 10 a.m.–12 a.m., Thursday–Saturday 10 a.m.–3 a.m.

Qdoba Mexican Grill
Food: Mexican
3712 Forbes Ave.
(412) 802-7866
Price: $6–$12 per person
Hours: Sunday–Wednesday 10:30 a.m.–11 p.m., Thursday–Saturday 10:30 a.m.–12 a.m.

Quaker Steak & Lube Express
Food: Wings
3600 Forbes Ave., Oakland
(412) 246-4465
Price: $8–$15 per person
Hours: Sunday–Thursday 11 a.m.–10 p.m., Friday–Saturday 11 a.m.–11 p.m.

Ritters Diner
Food: Diner fare
5221 Baum Blvd., Shadyside
(412) 682-4852
Cool Features: Very clean for a local diner.
Hours: Daily 24 hours

Sushi Too
Food: Japanese
5432 Walnut St., Shadyside
(412) 687-8744
www.sushi2-too.com
Price: $7–$15 per person
Hours: Monday–Thursday 11:30 a.m.–3 p.m., and 5 p.m.–10 p.m.,
Friday 11:30 a.m.–3 p.m. and 5 p.m.–11 a.m.,
Saturday 11:30 a.m.–11 p.m.,
Sunday 1 p.m.–9 p.m.

Thai Place Café
Food: Thai
301 S. Craig St., Oakland
(412) 622-0133
www.thaiplacepgh.com
Cool Features: Lunch specials. Award-winning Thai restaurant in Pittsburgh.
Price: $6–$15 per person
Hours: Monday–Saturday 10:30 a.m.–9:30 p.m., Sundays closed

Uncle Sam's Gourmet Subs
210 Oakland Ave.
(412) 621-1885
Price: $4–$9 per person

(Uncle Sams, continued)
Cool Features: Award-winning subs.
Hours: Monday–Friday 10:30 a.m.–8:30 p.m., Saturday 11 a.m.–8 p.m., Sunday 11 a.m.–6 p.m.

Union Grill
Food: American
413 S. Craig St., Oakland
(412) 681-8620
Cool Features: Outdoor dining, good happy hour specials.
Price: $7–$15 per person
Hours: Sunday–Thursday 11 a.m.–10 p.m., Friday–Saturday 11 a.m.–11 p.m.

Village Pizza
Food: Pizza, Italian
810 Ivy St., Shadyside
(412) 682-6878
Cool Features: Six packs sold until 2 a.m.
Price: $2–$10 per person

(Village Pizza, continued)
Hours: Monday–Tuesday 11 a.m.–12 a.m., Wednesday–Saturday 11 a.m.–2 a.m., Sunday 12 p.m.–2 a.m.

Vocelli Pizza
Food: Pizza
3608 Fifth Ave., Oakland
412.687.4666
www.vocellipizza.com
Price: $8–$12 per person
Hours: Sunday–Thursday 11 a.m.–2 a.m., Friday–Saturday 11 a.m.–3 a.m.

Wing Pitt
Food: Wings, salads, sandwiches
424 Semple St.
(412) 681-8608
Price: $4–$30
Hours: Monday–Thursday 11 a.m.–11 p.m., Friday–Saturday 11 a.m.–12 a.m., Sunday 12 p.m.–10 p.m.

Did You Know?

Local favorite Primanti Brothers' restaurant puts a twist on the average sandwich by placing both the **french fries and coleslaw between the bun**, a touch that has become known as unique to Pittsburgh-style sandwiches.

Hemingway's and Fuel & Fuddle, which are both heavily Pitt-centered, tend to host **music, poetry readings, or group gatherings**.

Student Favorites:
Fuel & Fuddle
Hemingway's Café
India Garden
Joe Mama's
Union Grill

Late-Night, Half-Price Food Specials:
Hemingway's Café, after 9 p.m.
India Garden from 4 p.m.–6 p.m., and 10 p.m.–1 a.m.
Mad Mex, after 9 p.m.
Union Grill, after 10 p.m.
Pittsburgh Deli Co., after 10 p.m.
Fuel and Fuddle, after 11 p.m.
Joe Mama's, after 11 p.m.

24-Hour Eating:
Eat 'n Park
Ritter's Diner

Closest Grocery Stores:
Giant Eagle
4612 Centre Ave., Oakland
(412) 681-1500

Giant Eagle
4250 Murray Ave., Squirrel Hill
(412) 421-8161

Best Pizza:
Vocelli Pizza

Best Chinese:
Lulu's Noodle Shop, and Yum Wok

Best Breakfast:
Pamela's

Best Wings:
Wing Pitt

Best Healthy:
Panera Bread

Best Place to Take Your Parents:
Joe Mama's Italian Delux and Hard Rock Café

Other Places to Check Out:
Aladdin's Eatery, Cheese Cellar Café, Five Guys Famous Burgers & Fries, Gullifty's, La Fiesta Restaurant, McDonald's, Napoli Pizzeria, Peter's Pub, Qdoba Mexican Grill, Spice Island Tea House, Subway, Sushi Boat, Vera Cruz Tienda Mexicana, Wendy's

Students Speak Out On...
Off-Campus Dining

"Pittsburgh has some great places to eat. Primanti Brothers is unique, and famous for their huge sandwiches with coleslaw, fries, and anything else you like all piled high on bread. There's also great Italian food. The variety is definitely here."

Q "There are good restaurants. My absolute favorite, Mad Mex, has half-off food everyday after 11 p.m., half-off margaritas everyday between 10–11 p.m., and happy hour and specials for lunch. Fuel & Fuddle is a nice restaurant/bar—they also have half-off food after 11 p.m., as does Joe Mama's. These places are all in Oakland, just blocks from the dorms, and are crowded every night, because all college kids are poor. **Half-off food is sweet**!"

Q "There are **a ton of restaurants around the dorms**. There are regular fast-food places, like Wendy's and McDonald's, and there are also restaurants like Uncle Sam's, for steak sandwiches and such, and Fuel & Fuddle—these are my two favorites."

Q "There are way too many restaurants to mention. There are many good ones, and they represent all types of food. There's Joe Mama's for Italian, Uncle Sam's for subs, and Fuel & Fuddle for various dishes. Farther off campus, **Cozumel is great for Mexican**, Gullifty's is good for awesome desserts, and the Cheese Cellar offers a nicer dining experience."

Q "There's a ton of places around campus. **Pittsburgh is really good for ethnic foods**, like Chinese, Indian, and Mexican."

Q "There's pretty much everything you can think of as far as fast food is concerned. There are a few spots where we go to eat that are nicer college hangouts—Fuel & Fuddle is the big one. After 11 p.m., everything is half price, and it's always packed. It's **good food, and right on campus.**"

Q "Two words: half price! Hemingway's, Joe Mama's, Fuel & Fuddle and several other places are half price for several menu items after 11 p.m. If you don't like cigarette smoke, Hemingway's and Fuel and Fuddle might be a problem, since after 11 p.m., there's **virtually no non-smoking section.**"

Q "There are many places to eat because the campus spreads out across a large area. Basically, **you can get anything, including stuff like sushi and Middle Eastern cuisine**. It all depends on what you like to eat."

Q "The restaurants on campus aren't that great, but there are a lot of fast food places, and international cuisine places nearby. **Check out the Spice Island Tea House.** The bus line also hits downtown Pittsburgh, and all of the great places near there."

Q "Restaurants are good. Near or on campus, there are good college spots like Fuel & Fuddle, Hemingway's, and Peter's Pub. Off campus, you can go all over the city by bus for any type of food. There are lots of ethnic foods, too, from Indian to Thai to Chinese. **The Sushi Boat has really good Japanese food.**"

Q "Being in a city means lots of diverse people, and they all have their own restaurants. Pittsburgh is an ethnic town with ethnic restaurants offering Indian, Japanese, Lebanese, Italian, Polish, Chinese, and French food. The city buses are free for Pitt students, so it's easy to get everywhere. There are also a lot of other restaurants, especially pizza places. Most of the **really nice, expensive places are on Mount Washington and in downtown Pittsburgh.**"

Q "The 'O' is ranked third best among hot dog joints in America, I think, and their fries are incredible. **Off-campus dining is accessible through the school's bus service**, or, if you want to go further away, through the city bus system. McDonald's, Wendy's, and Subway are also about two minutes away from the most populated dorms."

Q "There are **a zillion great places to eat off campus** in a five- to ten-minute bus ride. Try Fuel & Fuddle or Uncle Sam's right near campus. Joe Mama's has good Italian, and Qdoba and La Fiesta have great Mexican. Try Yum Wok/Lu-Lu's Noodles for pan Asian food."

Q "If you hop a bus, you can go to one of the best Thai restaurants in the country on Walnut Street in Shadyside. If you head to Squirrel Hill, **you can hit Aladdin's for great Middle Eastern Cuisine** on Forbes Avenue, or Napoli for some of the best pizza in the city on Murray Avenue. And that's without venturing far off campus!"

Q "There is Joe Mama's for Italian, India Garden for Indian, and Mad Mex for Mexican. Not to mention the famous Primanti Brothers or Fuel and Fuddle for the American appetite. The best thing is that most of these have **reduced menus after 11 o'clock**."

The College Prowler Take On...
Off-Campus Dining

Whatever your taste, you're bound to find it around Pittsburgh—in most cases, right near Pitt's campus. There is an impressive selection of restaurants in Oakland that cater to college students with late-night, half-price menus and drink specials. Beyond the usual fast food fare, there are quite a few independent and unique eateries nestled around Forbes Avenue, and in South Oakland. The same is true of Craig Street, a favorite area just two blocks away from the Cathedral of Learning. Nearby Shadyside also has a lot of options, including many ethnic restaurants and coffee shops, however, the whole area is generally pricier than Oakland. Add to these the number of restaurants in Squirrel Hill, downtown, South Side, and other neighborhoods—all of which can be reached in a 10 to 15 minute bus ride—and student choices skyrocket. Many of the places close to Pitt realize that their clientele is mostly college students, and have pricing, menus, and hours to suit. Long after the University's dining halls have closed, students favorites such as Hemingway's, Fuel & Fuddle, and Mad Mex all stay open as late as 2 a.m. The 'O' is almost always open, and is a traditional hangout after the bars close.

It's a great idea to take weekends with friends and explore the neighborhoods around the area; ask upperclassmen for the best places to check out. There are many hidden treasures, often with very good prices and excellent food. The Spice Island Tea House, for example, is hidden among townhouses just a few blocks off campus, but has some of the best Southeast Asian cuisine in the city. If there's one thing Pitt students can't complain about, it's the tremendous dining scene right at their doorstep.

The College Prowler® Grade on

Off-Campus Dining: A

A high Off-Campus Dining grade implies that off-campus restaurants are affordable, accessible, and worth visiting. Other factors include the variety of cuisine and the availability of alternative options (vegetarian, vegan, Kosher, etc.).

Campus Housing

The Lowdown On...
Campus Housing

Best Dorms:
Forbes Hall
Sutherland Hall

Worst Dorms:
Litchfield Towers
Lothrop Hall

Room Types:
Single, double, triple, or quadruple, with communal or semi-private bathrooms
Suite-style (5 to 8 students), with semi-private bathroom

Undergrads Living on Campus:
44%

Number of Dormitories:
12

Number of University-Owned Apartments:
4

Dormitories:

Amos Hall
Floors: 11
Total Occupancy: 153
Bathrooms: Shared by suite
Coed: No, all women
Residents: Mostly upperclassmen
Room Types: Singles and doubles with common living areas
Special Features: Made up of sorority suites, laundry facilities in penthouse, kitchens and chapter rooms in all suites, 24-hour fitness center on ground floor

Brackenridge Hall
Floors: 11
Total Occupancy: 206
Bathrooms: Shared by suite
Coed: Yes
Residents: Mostly upperclassmen
Room Types: 4- and 5-person suites, several singles and doubles
Special Features: Laundry facilities in penthouse, MicroFridges in almost every room

Bruce Hall
Floors: 11
Total Occupancy: 196
Bathrooms: Shared by suite
Coed: Yes
Residents: Mostly upperclassmen

(Bruce Hall, continued)
Room Types: 4-, 5-, 6-, and 8-person suites
Special Features: International living units available, laundry facilities on every floor, kitchenette and fridge in each suite, 7-11 located on street level of same building

Forbes Hall
Floors: 6
Total Occupancy: 232
Bathrooms: Some communal, some shared by doubles, all communal showers
Coed: Yes
Residents: Freshmen and upperclassmen
Room Types: Doubles, triples
Special Features: Air conditioned, study rooms, two kitchenettes and laundry facilities on every floor, large recreation and study area, free pool and Ping-Pong, patio, select triples have balconies

Holland Hall
Total Occupancy: 600
Bathrooms: Communal
Coed: No, all women
Room Types: Singles, doubles, triples, quads
Residents: Freshmen and upperclassmen
Special Features: Kitchenette on each floor, 24-hour quiet floors available, lounge, study area, laundry facilities in penthouse

Litchfield Towers

Floors: Tower A – 19, Tower B – 22, Tower C – 16

Total Occupancy: Tower A – 660, Tower B – 765, Tower C – 435

Bathrooms: Communal

Coed: Yes

Residents: Mostly freshmen

Room Types: Singles, doubles

Special Features: Air conditioned, 24-hour quiet floors available, 24-hour fitness center; Towers A and B are all-freshman housing

Lothrop Hall

Floors: 14

Total Occupancy: 698

Bathrooms: Communal, a few semi-private

Coed: Yes

Residents: Freshmen and upperclassmen

Room Types: Singles, a few doubles and quads

Special Features: 24-hour quiet floors available, sinks in most rooms, study lounges, 24-hour fitness center

McCormick Hall

Floors: 11

Total Occupancy: 167

Bathrooms: Private and semi-private

Coed: Yes

Residents: Mostly upperclassmen

(McCormick Hall, continued)

Room Types: 5-, 6-, 7-, and 8-person suites

Special Features: Lounge and recreation area on first floor, laundry facilities in penthouse

Pennsylvania Hall

Total Occupancy: 420

Bathrooms: Private, or shared by suite

Coed: Yes

Residents: Upperclassmen

Room Types: Doubles and 4-person suites

Special Features: Lounge and study room on each floor, air-conditioned rooms, laundry facilities on each floor, fitness center on ground floor, Honors College Living and Learning Community

Sutherland Hall

Total Occupancy: 768

Bathrooms: Communal and semi-private

Coed: Yes

Room Types: Mostly doubles with semi-private baths, some triples with shared baths, and a limited number of suites

Residents: Freshmen and upperclassmen

Special Features: Air conditioned, adjacent to athletic facilities, TV/study lounge on every floor, cafeteria, convenience store, computer center, mailroom, laundry facilities on ground floor, Honors College Living and Learning Community

Apartment-style Housing:

Bouquet Gardens (8 buildings)
Location: South Bouquet St.
Total Occupancy: 496
Bathrooms: Semi-private (2 per apartment)
Coed: Yes
Room Types: All apartments include 4 bedrooms, a kitchen, living room, and dining area
Special Features: Air conditioned, full kitchen

Centre Plaza Apartments
Location: 5032 Centre Ave.
Total Occupancy: 197
Bathrooms: Semi-private
Coed: Yes
Room Types: All apartments house 1–3 students and feature full kitchens, dinettes, and common area
Special Features: Air conditioned, equipped kitchen

Forbes Craig Apartments
Location: 4351 Forbes Ave.
Total Occupancy: 102
Bathrooms: Semi-private
Coed: Yes

(Forbes Craig Apartments, continued)
Room Types: All apartments house 2–3 students (single or double bedrooms), and feature a kitchen and common area
Special Features: Forbes Craig housing is restricted to University Honors College students, laundry facilities, limited student parking available, pool table

Oakwood Apartments
Location: 234/236 Oakland Ave.
Total Occupancy: 38
Bathrooms: Semi-private
Coed: Yes
Room Types: All apartments house 1–2 students, feature a kitchen and common area
Special Features: Limited student parking is available

Housing Offered:
Singles: 22%
Doubles: 43%
Triples/Suites: 21%
Apartments: 14%

Bed Type
Extra-long twin

Available for Rent
MicroFridge (mini-fridge with microwave)

What You Get
A bed, desk and chair, closet, dresser, window dressings, phone, cable jack, Ethernet hookups

Also Available
Extended cable, specialized living areas

Cleaning Service?
In public areas. Community bathrooms are cleaned daily Monday–Friday. Apartment-style living spaces, and semi-private bathrooms are not cleaned by the staff.

Did You Know?

Pitt's newest residence hall on the upper campus is expected to be completed for the 2006–2007 academic year. The coed building will be home to 513 students in both doubles and three- and five-person suites with private bathrooms, as well as a fitness center and coffee bar on the ground floor. Students can access a Web cam that follows the building's construction through the residence life Web site at: *www.pc.pitt.edu/housing/p_cam.html*.

The student union used to be an all-male residence hall. Mike Ditka lived there when he attended Pitt.

Students Speak Out On...
Campus Housing

"**The dorms aren't that special. My first year in Lothrop Hall sucks. It's old, there is no air-conditioning, and right on top is a helicopter pad. Every night, the hospital helicopter takes off and lands a ton of times; it doesn't exactly help you sleep.**"

Q "Lothrop is the place to be if you want a single room; Brackenridge is very nice for suites. Lothrop, Towers, and Amos all have gyms in them, and other buildings in the quad are just a hop away. Sutherland has a computer lab and an all-you-can-eat cafeteria in it; though, it's way up a hill on the other side of campus; most athletes live there. Holland is an all-girls dorm, and it also houses a lot of freshmen. **Towers is the center of the action; most freshmen are in Towers**, and the floors never sleep."

Q "The residence halls are very good, for the most part. The Towers are at the low end of places to live while Bouquet Gardens are probably the best, but where you live depends a lot on your year. **Most rooms have plenty of space** in the various residence halls. Towers would be the worst, mostly because they are the smallest, but they're the major freshman dorms and a great place to meet people."

Q "As a freshman, you'll probably be placed in the Towers—they are three circular high-rises. One has 22 floors, one has 19, and the other has 21; they are all connected by one lobby. There's always a bunch of people in there, and always something going on. I stayed in Tower B; it's a **great way to meet people**."

Q "It's pretty good. The Towers are best for freshmen—you'll meet more people there, even if **the rooms are a little shady**."

Q "Dorms for freshmen tend to suck at any school. The **Towers are pretty lame**—Sutherland is nice, and a fair number of freshmen live there."

Q "All of the dorms are good. If possible, avoid the Towers. It's not that they're bad; it's just that people who aren't used to sharing space with a roomie might get freaked out by the close quarters. **Try for Sutherland, Forbes, or Lothrop for the nicest dorm rooms**."

Q "For freshmen, I would suggest the Towers. I know **they look, smell, and feel awful**, but it really is the best way to meet people. I lived in Holland Hall my freshman year. I wasn't crammed into a pie-shaped room, but I also didn't get the chance to meet as many people."

Q "I've never lived in Sutherland, but I've seen the rooms, and they're some of the nicest on campus, right along with Forbes Hall. Both of these halls are rather far from the center of campus, but they are on the shuttle line. **Sutherland is air conditioned, and has its own cafeteria** and computer lab for convenience. Tower C is great if you want a single room, especially since it's been newly renovated with new furniture, bathrooms, carpeting, lounges, and it has air-conditioning."

Q "Compared to what I've seen at other colleges, **dorm life at Pitt isn't really that bad**. There are different options for housing beyond the 'normal' floors—honors housing, alcohol-free floors, 24-hour quiet floors, and single-major floors, just to name a few. Facilities are entirely livable, but, I can't imagine why anyone would spend more than their first two years living on campus."

Q "All the residence halls are nice but different, and depending on what you're looking for, and where you want to be, there are plenty of options. For instance, nursing and med students could stay in Lothrop—right in the heart of UPMC—or Forbes Hall, which is close to Forbes Tower. If you are a freshman, you live in Towers. It's not mandatory, but it's the most fun you'll ever have in the dorms, plus it's **where a lot of people meet their friends** during first year."

Q "The Towers are the place people remember most about Pitt. They're round buildings with pie-shaped rooms. Two towers have double rooms, and the other has singles. I stayed in a single in Towers, and it was a hell hole, but if I hadn't stayed there, I'd regret it. The **lobby of the Towers is a huge congregation area**, with two cafeterias below. Right outside of the lobby is the 'Ashtray,' where everyone goes to smoke—both freshmen and upperclassmen (smoking is prohibited in all the dorms)."

Q "When I was a freshman, we got to request which building we lived in—not that many people got what they wanted, but now I think you can just request how many roommates you want. There's **a lot of variety among the places offered**, but wherever you live, just do your best to be social and meet people. The people you live with will probably be your closest friends."

Q "Dorm life is dorm life. I don't think you should really avoid any special dorm. If you can get into Bouquet Gardens or Sutherland Hall, they're both nice. The quad is super convenient, and **you can usually get a suite with your friends**."

Q "All of the dorms are nice for their own reason, but you have to be careful because **they don't all have air-conditioning**. The Schenley quad is my favorite because all of the buildings are old and have a lot of personality."

The College Prowler Take On...
Campus Housing

Every residence hall at Pitt has its own distinct perks and downfalls. When you first get to Pitt, you'll find the majority of your class living in Towers A or B, which are all-freshman housing. Many upperclassmen see the Towers as "the most fun you'll never want to have again." The best thing about these dorms is that all residents are in the same boat—this makes it a great place to meet people and make friends during your first year. On the other hand, the rooms are small, without air-conditioning, and pie-shaped, (the Towers are actually circular high-rises). Some students say that this adds character, while others end up feeling like they're housed in a sardine can. If all-freshman living isn't your cup of tea, there are a few other options available for first-years. If you're a female, Holland Hall offers a more spacious alternative, and is right next door to Towers. You still won't have air-conditioning, but you will be right on the quad, close to everything. Forbes and Sutherland are universally regarded as the best dorms on campus, but they are also the farthest from everything. If you live in either of these, you'll either learn to love walking up hills or spend a lot of time waiting for shuttles.

Overall, the residence halls are well maintained. One of the biggest complaints is that the housing staff does not clean semi-private or private bathrooms, only communal areas. Students have also mentioned that hallways aren't always swept, and housing tends to keep quiet about the fact that you can borrow vacuum cleaners from many of the main desks at residence halls. Every dorm is outfitted with 24-hour security service, and you must be a building resident in order to get in. This keeps Pitt housing feeling very safe, but many students agree that it also makes simple tasks, such as having friends visit, much more difficult—you have to sign everyone in and out. While you probably won't find the height of your college experience living on campus, you can be sure that one of the halls has an environment you'll be able to deal with during your first years.

C+

The College Prowler® Grade on Campus Housing: C+

A high Campus Housing grade indicates that dorms are clean, well-maintained, and spacious. Other determining factors include variety of dorms, proximity to classes, and social atmosphere.

Off-Campus Housing

The Lowdown On...
Off-Campus Housing

Undergrads in Off-Campus Housing:
56%

Best Time to Look for a Place:
Early spring semester

Average Rent For:
Studio Apt.: $400/month
1BR Apt.: $500/month
2BR Apt.: $700/month

Popular Areas:
Bloomfield
North Oakland
Shadyside
South Oakland
Squirrel Hill

For Assistance Contact:
Housing Resource Center
127 North Bellefield Avenue
(412) 624-6998
www.pitt.edu/~property

Students Speak Out On...
Off-Campus Housing

> "Most houses are really close. I am living off campus next year, and it shouldn't be too bad. If you are lucky, you can get a close apartment; if not, there are shuttles and city buses to help you."

Q "There is a ton of off-campus housing available, and many **very convenient to campus**. Pitt does a good job of providing information on local landlords, and teaching students what to look for before signing a lease."

Q "There are lots of houses and apartments for rent; you just have to get to them early. Most are **nowhere near as nice as the on-campus apartments**. Dorms are a different story."

Q "There's off-campus housing all over the place, and it's mainly used by college students around Pitt. If you wait until the fall to look, though, you probably would have a **hard time finding a place**."

Q "It's very convenient. I live off campus, yet I'm never more than **five to ten minutes from my classes**."

Q "It actually **works out more cheaply to live off campus**. Some of the South Oakland apartments can be kind of run down, but most students live in North Oakland, where the nicer, upper-scale apartments are."

Q "It was fun living in South Oakland. Look for a place in advance, and you're fine. **Some places are dumpy**, but you can get something affordable and nice nearby."

Q "Make sure you look at places other than North or South Oakland. North can be a strange area, and **South Oakland is one of the loudest and most run-down neighborhoods** for students. It's not bad, as long as you know what you're getting. Up by CMU, and near the Shadyside, Squirrel Hill, or Bloomfield areas, however, you can get really nice places for a better price—you just have to be willing to take a bus to class."

Q "Off-campus housing is very convenient. Most people who live off campus live in North or South Oakland, a five to **20-minute walk, depending on where you live, but there are buses**. There are lots of other places around the city to live. I know a lot of people who live in Shadyside, Squirrel Hill, Southside, and Lawrenceville. They all just get a bus to and from campus."

Q "Off-campus housing can save you money, but you have to search diligently for a good place. It's not that easy to find a good spot, and the **demands for the nicer places are really high**. If you look for a place ahead of time, you'll be fine."

Q "You're guaranteed housing through your junior year if you turn in your housing deposit on time—so make sure you do that. A lot of students tend to live on campus for at least two years just because once you move off campus, depending on where you live, **you tend not to see as many of your friends** and people from your classes as you did before. Plus, it's convenient to live on campus for a lot of people, and the best part is that you can get a place in Bouquet Gardens. Many students will try and live there because you have the benefits if living in an apartment, with the convenience of living on campus."

Q "It's definitely cheaper to live off campus and **buy a commuter meal plan**, but if you want to live off campus, you have to search for an apartment rather early before all the good locations are rented. Stay away from South Oakland; everyone calls it 'the Dirty South' for a reason."

Q "**Off-campus housing can be fun** if you know what you're willing to pay, and what you'll get for what you're willing to pay. If you don't want to pay a lot, you usually won't get the Taj Mahal. Sometimes you get lucky."

Q "You have to realize that you need to have a good sense of humor about an off-campus apartment. **Things break, neighbors can suck, landlords can be shady**; but if you keep your sense of humor, you can get things fixed, make nice with the neighbors, and learn how to get what you need from your landlord. Off-campus housing can be as conveniently located as you like—a five-minute walk, a five-minute bus ride, or even farther. It's all what you want!"

Q "There are a decent amount of people who do move off campus sophomore year, for freedom's sake. Personally, I am lazy, so **I like living on campus**, but off-campus housing is also close, and relatively easy to find."

The College Prowler Take On...
Off-Campus Housing

The key to finding a great place off campus is to scour the area as much as possible. There are so many options that it isn't uncommon to stumble across the perfect place; at the same time, however, it's also not difficult to find places that are way too expensive or have "slum lord" property managers. There are two main areas that Pitt students tend to live off campus: North and South Oakland. Students joke about South Oakland being "the ghetto"—it's a little more run-down than the rest of Oakland, and it's a little louder and less safe. The houses and apartments there, however, tend to be much more affordable, and therefore attractive to the college crowd. North Oakland has nicer places in a better area, but you're not always getting what you pay for. As you move farther away from campus, options increase, and prices vary more. Shadyside, next to North Oakland, is considered the best area in which to live. Rent prices reflect this, with rates almost doubling those in South Oakland. Squirrel Hill can be the best of both worlds, with nice apartments and reasonable rents; of all the neighborhoods Pitt students usually move to, however, this one is farthest out.

The best advice is to start looking early. If you haven't found an apartment by March—good luck. The best places get snatched up quickly. Your options are also going to increase by a lot if you have roommates. Some of the best areas are mainly house rentals, which are entirely affordable if you have three or four other people that you can share a living space with. For better apartments, even having one or two roommates will lower your rent significantly. Read everything before you sign any leases, and, most importantly, get to know the area where you're looking to rent. Pittsburgh neighborhoods have a lot to offer, but it's best to know what you're getting into ahead of time.

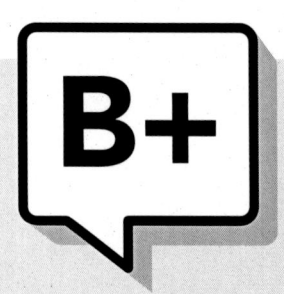

B+

The College Prowler® Grade on
Off-Campus Housing: B+

A high grade in Off-Campus Housing indicates that apartments are of high quality, close to campus, affordable, and easy to secure.

Diversity

The Lowdown On...
Diversity

Native American:
Less than 1%

African American:
9%

Asian American:
4%

Hispanic:
1%

White:
85%

International:
1%

Out-of-State:
15%

Political Activity

Political activity is abundant around campus; however, only a small portion of students actually involve themselves in it. There are many different clubs and organizations for political causes that students can become involved in. The Student Government Board (SGB) is one highly sought-after organization and works as the hub of campus politics.

Gay Pride

Pitt students are generally accepting of people with any lifestyle. There are a number of homosexual student groups through campus acting to raise awareness and foster a better environment for the gay and lesbian community. A few gay bars also exist in the area.

Most Popular Religions

There are a few religious organizations throughout the campus. Although much of the campus considers itself Christian or Catholic, the most predominant religious organization on campus is the Jewish organization, and there is also a sizable Jewish population on Pitt's campus.

Economic Status

There are students from every possible economic background you could imagine. Money is not something openly discussed between students, and it is not really an issue across the campus.

Minority Clubs

There are plenty of minority clubs on campus, including the Asian Student Association, the Black Action Society, and the Rainbow Alliance, to name a few. Minority clubs hold a strong presence on campus and are becoming more and more well known and diverse as the years go by.

Students Speak Out On...
Diversity

"**The campus is very diverse, due in large part to its urban setting and strong research programs, which attract foreign students.** It's a very good opportunity to absorb different cultures, if you choose to do so."

Q "I don't think the campus is really all that diverse—**most of the people here are white**."

Q "**The diversity is impressive**, especially within the science and engineering departments. Those areas attract a lot of foreign students."

Q "It's **probably the most diverse place I've seen**—it's great. Then again, I am from rural Pennsylvania, and my standard for diversity is kind of low."

Q "We have every kind of group, from the Rainbow Alliance (for gays and bisexuals), to the Black Action Society. There are political parties, **fights against hunger, religious groups**, and other things. There is a lot of diversity among the students here."

Q "There are a lot of minorities on campus, but it might not seem like it because there's a tendency to stick with your own. There are several diversity organizations, such as Theta Nu Xi multicultural sorority, but the **diversity of your social circle really depends on you**."

Q **"If you have led a sheltered life, you will be freaked out** when you come here. We have gays, lesbians, goths, and preps. Pretty much any type of person you can think of. We also have foreigners."

Q "Pitt's campus seems fairly diverse. While there is definitely a white majority, it seems like we have a pretty good sampling of all ethnic groups on the main campus. The Honors College, however, is another story—I live in the honors housing, and participate in some activities offered through the **Honors College, and there is a definite lack of diversity** within these groups."

Q "As a city, Pittsburgh is not as diverse as it may seem. We are in western Pennsylvania, which does not attract a lot of different cultures and races. Just the same, there are **a number of international students on Pitt's campus**, as well as on other college campuses in the area. If you look around closely, you will find a lot of diversity, though, it's not right in your face like in New York or Washington, DC."

Q "Pittsburgh might seem diverse because of the school down the block, Carnegie Mellon, but besides that, it really isn't. **The University of Pittsburgh is known for treating minorities unfairly**, especially African Americans."

Q "Pitt needs a lot of help with improving their relations with African Americans on campus, and **representation from other ethnicities is extremely low** for us being in a so-called major city."

Q "It's not that diverse over here. Mostly, everyone here is from somewhere in Pennsylvania, and **the majority of the campus is white**. If you're from a big city, you'll think this place isn't diverse at all, but if you're from the middle of nowhere, you might be impressed."

Q "I think that campus diversity has leapt forward a lot in the time that I've been a student here. **Come to Pitt with an open mind**—be appreciative that other people live their lives differently. I think you can find a lot of people from every walk of life here at Pitt! Appreciate what you can learn from those cultures different from yours!"

Q "There's **one of every type of person here at Pitt**, even though I wouldn't say that it is the most diverse campus religiously or racially. Some of the groups on campus that are race- or religion-oriented seem to defeat their purpose. They always claim that they help those within their group to 'fit in better with the rest of the students,' but they do exactly the opposite. Organizations like that only help to segregate the campus, not unite it. If you're looking for an incredibly diverse place to go, Pitt may not be what you're looking for."

Q "The school tries to make the campus comfortable for people from all walks of life. The minorities on campus are very active. Personally, I know my own group of friends is pretty diverse. The only problem is that **the diverse groups don't intermingle much**."

The College Prowler Take On...
Diversity

Diversity is a very subjective area for Pitt students, and what you hear really depends on who you talk to. Numbers speak for themselves—there is a large white majority at the University, and many people are from Pennsylvania or the surrounding areas. If you're coming to Pittsburgh from one of its many suburbs, you'll probably be impressed with the number of different people you can find. The same is true of the Oakland area, which is home to a lot of schools that are even more diverse than Pitt. For those from other cities or very diverse areas, however, the University itself may seem depressingly homogenous.

While diversity isn't a major issue around campus, there are many student groups available for minorities to gather and hold activities, promote causes, and socialize. In addition to groups based strictly on ethnicity, there is also a wide range of interests covered by these clubs. Religion, politics, athletics, music, and hobbies are all very diverse areas around Pitt, and these can sometimes be the best way to make new friends. You'll find that students have a huge range of backgrounds and beliefs, and there really are many niches to fall into. If you want to have a diverse social circle, it's entirely possible at Pitt; you may just have to look a little harder than the people you first run into on move-in day.

The College Prowler® Grade on
Diversity: C

A high grade in Diversity indicates that ethnic minorities and international students have a notable presence on campus and that students of different economic backgrounds, religious beliefs, and sexual preferences are well-represented.

Guys & Girls

The Lowdown On...
Guys & Girls

Men Undergrads:
48%

Women Undergrads:
52%

Birth Control Available?

Yes, pills, patches, the shot, as well as condoms, are available through Student Health Services.

Social Scene

The social scene is largely what you make it. If you want to party, Pitt has plenty of opportunities to do so, every day of the week. Between campus activities, fraternity parties, house parties, and other venues, you can easily be a social butterfly, if that's what you want. The city also offers a good bit in the way of cultural activities and entertainment that isn't school-affiliated. Check local bulletin boards, the *City Paper*, and online for activity postings.

Hookups or Relationships?

Both; hookups more so in your first two years, but relationships kick in as you get older and closer to graduation.

Best Place to Meet Guys/Girls

Hillman Library, for the most studious, as well as lecture classes (labs are helpful), and the cafeterias. South Oakland house parties and frat parties on the Hill seem to be the best place to meet the opposite sex outside of school buildings. For the older crowd, the local bars are packed, especially on Thursday, Friday, and Saturday nights. When the weather gets warm, you can always meet guys and girls who are hanging out on the Cathedral lawn, either studying, tanning, or playing a pick-up game of ultimate Frisbee.

Dress Code

Every style of clothing has its place around Pitt, but some are far more prevalent than others. Tank tops, shorts, and/or jeans for the girls are most popular during the warmer months. Guys tend toward T-shirts or polo shirts and khakis. During the winter, sweats are popular.

Did You Know?

Top Places to Find Hotties:
1. The Hill
2. Peter's Pub
3. Hillman Library

Top Places to Hook Up:
1. Cathedral stairways
2. Fraternity houses
3. Schenley Park
4. The Ashtray
5. Towers

Students Speak Out On...
Guys & Girls

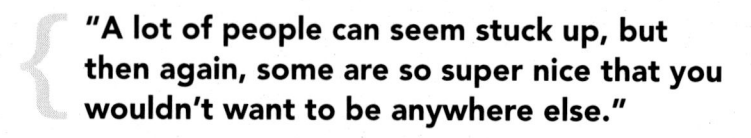

> "A lot of people can seem stuck up, but then again, some are so super nice that you wouldn't want to be anywhere else."

Q "There are enough attractive people of both genders to go around. The variety's not too bad—there are jocks, punks, skaters, and many more. **I've had my share of male distractions**."

Q "Most people are nice. They don't really care what you do, unless they know you. There are **plenty of hot people on campus**, but it doesn't matter if you're hot or not. People are either going to be nice or mean. Most likely, they will be nice."

Q "Guys and girls both seem pretty average on campus—there certainly isn't anything to complain about, really, but there does seem like an **inordinately large population of stereotypical sorority girls**."

Q "There are **more girls at Pitt than boys**, but not by a big margin at all. However, the girls are probably better looking than the guys. It always seems as though city schools attract a lot of good-looking girls, and country schools attract a lot of good-looking guys."

Q "The guys are guys, and the girls are decent. There is a **mix of hot girls and not-so-hot ones**. I guess the same would go for the guys, but I really don't concentrate on them."

Q "Everyone is **pretty nice**. As far as looks go—it all just depends on what you're looking for."

Q "I know that **people from Carnegie Mellon come here in the spring to just look at the Pitt girls**. They're wonderful eye-candy."

Q "All the guys are cool—most of them, anyway. **There are a few jerks**. Most of the girls are easy to get along with. I'd say compared to other schools, there are tons of guys who are better looking than I am, but there are a lot of female hotties on campus to go around."

Q "There are lots of guys and girls, and many of them are hotties. It's funny, because some days, especially when the weather isn't too nice, **you won't see that many attractive girls**. Once that sun comes out, it's like everyone that's hot decides to come out and play."

Q "Pitt girls are known for being hot. The guys are equally attractive. It's really cool, because **there's a huge diversity among everyone**. There are the preppy frat boys, the thugs, the normal-looking guys, the punks, and emo-kids, to name a few."

Q "There are a lot of pretty girls at Pitt—a lot. The best place to see them all at once is at the Student Union. Take a break there between classes on a nice day and **just admire the view**."

Q "**Some people suck, and some don't**. This place isn't as cultured as San Fran or New York; it's more like a college town filled with all types of people from bums to rich kids, drunks to sobers, and the thin to the obese."

Q "I always had **a great time with the guys** on campus. I made a lot of great guy friends and dated a few sweethearts. There are plenty of attractive people on campus!"

Q "Yeah, the guys are attractive, if you are thinking superficially. **They tend to go into the woodwork** during the winter, though."

The College Prowler Take On...
Guys & Girls

There are enough students at Pitt to make for a smorgasbord of potential relationships—whatever type of relationship you're looking for. The student body varies widely; though, girls are almost universally considered better looking on the whole. Pitt men have much less to complain about than CMU students up the street, because they have so many more options available. On the whole, however, campus isn't especially notable for the amount of romantic interaction; while relationships aren't uncommon, they also aren't by any means the rule of Pitt's social scene. Casual dating and hookups are frequent, especially during the first couple years.

Most students find that, beyond the romantic front, it's not hard to find a great group of close friends around Pitt. With people from so many walks of life, that's no surprise. By the end of the first year, many students already have their future roommates picked and have staked out regular hangouts and activities. Pittsburgh is known for being one of the friendlier American cities, and many people find themselves so comfortable in Oakland's environment that they're hard-pressed to want to leave. The best advice is to meet as many people, and check out as many different places, as you possibly can—there is a lot more going on than meets the eye, and sometimes you'll be most comfortable in the groups or activities that seemed intimidating when you first arrived. It can take some time to get settled in, but once you do, you'll likely find yourself surrounded by people you genuinely get along with.

B-

The College Prowler® Grade on
Guys: B-

A high grade for Guys indicates that the male population on campus is attractive, smart, friendly, and engaging, and that the school has a decent ratio of guys to girls.

B

The College Prowler® Grade on
Girls: B

A high grade for Girls not only implies that the women on campus are attractive, smart, friendly, and engaging, but also that there is a fair ratio of girls to guys.

Athletics

The Lowdown On...
Athletics

Athletic Division:
Division I

Conference:
Big East

School Mascot:
Panther

School Colors:
Blue and Gold

Men's Varsity Sports:
Baseball
Basketball
Cross-Country
Football
Soccer
Swimming & Diving
Track & Field
Wrestling

Women's Varsity Sports:
Basketball
Cross-Country
Gymnastics
Soccer
Softball
Swimming & Diving
Tennis
Track & Field
Volleyball

Club Sports:
Crew
Cycling
Equestrian
Hockey
Lacrosse
Rugby
Soccer
Ultimate Frisbee
Volleyball

Intramurals:
Basketball (Recreational and Competitive)
Touch Football
Racquetball
Soccer (Indoor and Outdoor)
Ultimate Frisbee
Volleyball

Most Popular Sports
Football and basketball

Overlooked Teams
Baseball, softball, volleyball, swimming, lacrosse, and rugby are all teams that don't get very much campus attention.

Best Place to Take a Walk
Schenley Park

Getting Tickets

Football tickets are easy to come by, and they are cheap for students. At $30 a set, season tickets give students seating at every home football game. Get to Heinz Field early, however, because once the lower student section fills up, you have to head to the nosebleed section. Basketball tickets are also cheap—$35 for a set of season tickets; however, there are only a small number of student season tickets available. This has been a source of complaints by the students for the last few years. All other sporting events are free.

Fields and Facilities

The Charles L. Cost Center
One of the newest athletic facilities, the Cost Center is big enough inside to house a regulation football field, or nine tennis courts. It functions as an indoor facility for football, baseball, and softball teams.

Fitzgerald Field House
The Field House serves as the home for a few of Pitt's sports programs, notably volleyball, gymnastics, wrestling, and indoor track and field. The Panthers have access to nearly 8,600 pounds of free weights at this facility, as well as great locker rooms and other amenities for athletes.

Heinz Field
Located by Point State Park and the city's three rivers, Heinz Field is the home of the Pittsburgh Steelers. The facility is used for Panther football games, and the team even has their own expansive locker room. On game weekends, the University provides transportation downtown; you can also ride city buses free with your student ID.

(Fields and Facilities, continued)

Petersen Events Center

Built as the new home of Panther basketball, the Pete was completed in the spring of 2002. In addition to the basketball team, this arena is used for campus ceremonies, graduation, concerts, and other events. The concourse features several eateries that are open to students during the daytime and a large recreation area (free weights, exercise machines, aerobic equipment, and racquetball courts) that is available for students.

Trees Hall

Trees is the home of the Panther swimming and diving team, and it houses the main pools used at the University. There are two main gyms and two swimming pools, as well as great diving areas.

Trees Field

Home to the Panthers baseball team, this field has been renovated to include new major-league Astroturf for the infield, as well as good lighting. It also includes two all-purpose fields, which are used as additional practice areas.

Students Speak Out On...
Athletics

> "Pitt is definitely a football and basketball school, for sure. It's easy to get season tickets for football, but for basketball, good luck. IM football, rugby, and other sports are starting to attract a sizeable following as well."

Q "Varsity sports are big, I guess. People go to the football games, and since the basketball team made it to the Sweet Sixteen, it has become extremely popular. Other than that, I don't think sports are that big to people, unless you are on one of the teams. The same goes for IM sports. There are **a lot of different teams and choices**; there are also a lot of club sports."

Q "I don't know too much about the sports here. **Football games are well attended**, though."

Q "Varsity sports are huge on campus, especially football and basketball. During the fall, **students pack Heinz Field on Saturdays** and the Petersen Events Center during basketball season. Intramural sports are pretty big on campus, and the most popular ones are football and basketball. These sports offer regular seasons followed by the playoffs."

Q "Varsity football and basketball are very big on campus. **Tailgating at football games is a highlight of the fall**."

Q "IM sports on campus are available, if you're interested. If we don't have the team you're looking for, the good news is that **you can create your own**!"

Q "Football and basketball are pretty big. Football games are down in the Heinz Field where the Steelers play, and it's always a good time. **They built a huge new basketball stadium** and athletics facility; it's awesome. IM sports are okay, but nothing special. They're not really that big."

Q "Varsity sports are huge. Football and basketball top the list, but the hockey and swimming teams get large crowds compared to other schools. **Pitt offers a large number of IM sports** that compete with the local colleges. There are also several classes with emphasis on IM sports."

Q "I don't pay much attention to them, except when they're doing well. I think that's how most people are. **Everyone goes to football games**, though. I know a bunch of people in IM sports, and they all love it. I used to be an athlete in high school, but it doesn't really compel me to sign up for anything anymore."

Q "Sports are pretty big here—football and basketball have a big draw. It's not the end of the world if you don't attend the events or like the events. But **school spirit makes this place a good time**, so I recommend at least checking it out!"

Q "The biggest varsity sports on campus would definitely have to be football and basketball. Both teams are excellent, especially our basketball team. **It's easier to get student tickets for the football team** as opposed to the basketball team, just because of seating limitations in the Peterson Event Center."

Q "I know **we have a good football and basketball team**, but I'm not really into that kind of thing at all."

Q "Varsity sports seem to be significant on campus, at least in terms of football and basketball. All the guys in my dorm were upset when they tried to get **season tickets for basketball, and the Web site kept crashing**. If you're trying for those, I'd recommend just walking over to the Pete."

Q "Football and men's basketball continue to be entertaining events. **It's really great going to a Division I school** because it acts as a cohesive for the student body."

Q "Pitt does not tend to be quite as sports-oriented as many other large state schools. Over the past couple of seasons, however, more attention has been drawn to sports, particularly to football and basketball. With **new coaching and new facilities**, plus some really great players, these two sports have been getting a lot of attention recently."

Q "If varsity sports aren't your thing, all you have to do is walk by the Cathedral anytime from late August into mid-November and you'll find **30–40 guys and girls playing rugby or ultimate Frisbee**. There's something for everyone."

Q "The basketball team is incredibly up-and-coming. They have **made the March Madness tournament for six seasons in a row**. The football coach, Wannstadt, a former NFL coach, is sure to draw in some highly sought-after recruits for years to come."

The College Prowler Take On...
Athletics

Athletics are off-the-hook at the University of Pittsburgh. Pitt's football team is often ranked in the top 25 and goes to a bowl game virtually every year. The program is expected to go nowhere but up. With a positive season last year, the recruiting possibilities are high. The men's basketball team has been nationally ranked over the past three seasons and looks to have a bright future ahead of them. Other varsity sports don't have the same draw as these two teams, but Pitt athletics holds its own in nearly every area. Swimming and diving always does well but is largely overlooked, and the volleyball team had a great season, too.

For those who don't want to play on varsity teams, there are numerous IM and club sports at Pitt. Soccer, football, basketball, and volleyball are most popular among students. All of these are coed and run each semester with a final playoff session at the end of the season. Although there are a lot of IM sports, many students aren't aware of them; in fact, compared to the number of students that attend the University, participation in intramurals is remarkably low. If you're looking for something even less formal, there are often pick-up games of Frisbee or soccer around the Cathedral lawn, and it's never hard to find friends in the dorms looking to shoot hoops or toss around a football.

A-

The College Prowler® Grade on
Athletics: A-

A high grade in Athletics indicates that students have school spirit, that sports programs are respected, that games are well-attended, and that intramurals are a prominent part of student life.

Nightlife

The Lowdown On...
Nightlife

Club and Bar Prowler: Popular Nightlife Spots!

Club Crawler:

For Pittsburgh's size, there are a good number of clubs in the area, thanks to the concentration of universities located in the city. Still, it doesn't take long for these large venues to drop out of popularity and for new ones to spring up.

Déjà Vu Lounge

2106 Penn Ave., Strip District
(412) 434-1144
www.dejavuloungepa.com

Déjà Vu is a nice place to relax and unwind during the evenings, but can get pretty packed at night. It's a lounge/club with different rooms that play a mix of techno and top 40. On Fridays and Saturdays there they unveil the sushi bar, and there are specials almost every night of the week.

(Déjà Vu Lounge, continued)

The rest of Déjà Vu's drinks are some of the most expensive in the city, but the dress code isn't extremely restrictive. Many people begin their evenings out here, since there is only a cover on Wednesdays. You must be 21 to get in, but they're not too harsh on the carding.

Halo Café

1005 East Carson St.,
South Side

(412) 431-HALO

www.halocafepgh.com

One of many Pittsburgh churches rennovated into something—ahem—not so sacred, Halo Cafe is slightly more trendy than the average popular eaterys and bars in South Side. The club features three floors including a dance floor, a bar and lounge, and an indoor balcony that could have once been some sort of choir loft. Halo usually appeals to a more upscale dance club crowd than the rest of college student-invested East Carson Street, so drinks are more expensive, and the menu runs from the common to the eclectic.

Margarita Mama's

1 Station Square,
Station Square

(412) 434-8100

www.margaritamamas.net

This is a Mexican-themed club with an outdoor deck, pool tables, and four bars.

(Margarita Mama's, continued)

While they serve some food, and their drink specialty is frozen margaritas, Mama's is most popular for dancing. On Thursdays, college kids get free of admission with their student IDs, and the college night bikini contest pays $500 to the hottest girl willing to strut across a catwalk in only a two-piece . . . or to the gal who brings the loudest friends. Mama's is pretty competitive with the Matrix, which is located in the same building, so specials and covers are constantly changing.

The Matrix

1 Station Square Unit E7,
Station Square

(412) 261-2220

The Matrix combines four different rooms into one nightclub. Club Liquid plays Miami-style trance, Club Exit plays New York-style house, Club Goddess plays top 40 music and old-school hip hop, and Club Velvet plays Latin music that is slightly old. The Matrix gets very packed, but it is fun because you can switch your dance music depending on your mood. They have a dress code, and their biggest night is Thursday.

Saddle Ridge

4 Station Square Dr. E., Station Square

(412) 434-6858

www.saddleridge pittsburgh.com

Located near the Matrix in Station Square, Saddle Ridge is a country club featuring line-dancing bartenders, mediocre drink specials, and a mechanical bull. Though there is little mainstream music played at Saddle Ridge, many country-music lovers and even non-country music lovers drop by to give the boot-scoot 'n boogie a shot, at least once. There is no dress code, but Saddle Ridge is the only place in Pittsburgh you're bound to spot hundreds of cowboy hats and plaid shirts intermingled with flashy club wear.

Tequila Willies

1501 Smallman St.

Boardwalk Complex, Strip District

(412) 281-1585

www.pghnightlife.com/tw_home.php

Tequila Willies is located on Pittsburgh's Boardwalk, at the end of the Strip District. The bar's outdoor deck has a striking view of the river, offers several indoor and outdoor bars, and a massive dance floor with a DJ spinning top 40.

(Tequila Willies, continued)

One of the older Pittsburgh clubs on the Boardwalk, Tequilla Willies is not as popular as it was at its peak, but the club's location keeps its doors open as a weekend stop for Pittsburgh club hoppers on their way to other popular Boardwalk clubs, such as Level, Touch, Sports Rock, and Light.

The Upstage

3609 Forbes Ave., Oakland

(412) 682-2084

www.the-upstage.com

Though the Upstage is open every night of the week, their most popular night by far is Thursday's '80s night. The scene is commonly fueled by $1.50 well drinks and domestic bottles from 10 p.m. to 12 a.m., mainstream and underground '80s music, and a regular crowd of punk kids. Smokey, dark, and filled with seriously furious '80s dancers, the Upstage is a nice break from the usual Pittsburgh club fun.

Bar Prowler:

There are countless bars to choose from throughout the city, and there's a relatively large selection extremely close to campus. City buses can open up a wide range of venues, and the best way to explore is to hit popular areas and try new places yourself.

Boomerang's

3909 Forbes Ave., Oakland

(412) 578-8491

Usually filled with the spillover from Hemingways because it is located next door, Boomerang's offers $1 Yuengling's everyday, and something Hemingways does not have—a dance floor.

Hemingway's Café

3911 Forbes Ave., South Oakland

(412) 621-4100

Hemingway's has become an obsession with the University of Pittsburgh students. Every single night of the week, this joint is packed, with barely enough room to squeeze up to the bar for a drink. Friends meet and eat here multiple times a week, and the bartenders know their most frequent clientele by name. With nightly dollar-drink specials, a pool table, and a juke box, it's exactly what a college bar should be.

Mad Mex

370 Atwood St., South Oakland

(412) 681-5656

www.madmex.com

The place to go for giant margaritas and Mexican food. Thanks to popular student specials and happy hours, the place is usually packed with both Pitt and Carnegie Mellon kids.

(Mad Mex, continued)

On Fridays, many students come here to start their weekend at 4 p.m., when margaritas and beers are half off (until 6 p.m.). Things get even more packed later in the evening. From 9 p.m.–11 p.m., giant margaritas are $6; after 11 p.m., all food is half off.

Panther Hollow Inn

4611 Forbes Ave., North Oakland

(412) 682-0588

This is mostly a CMU hangout, but it's right up the street from Pitt. Weekday nights at PHI are packed because of the $4 pitcher deal during happy hour.

Peter's Pub

116 Oakland Ave., Oakland

(412) 681-7465

Located not more than a block or so from main campus, like Hemingway's, this bar is a place to relax and drink with friends, but by the time the nightly special is over, the dance floor is packed with drunkenly dancing students. Sometimes, Peter's is also known to host a local band behind their second-floor bar.

Pittsburgh Deli Company (PDC, The Deli)

728 Copeland St., Shadyside

(412) 682-3354

www.pghdeli.com

(Pittsburgh Deli Company, continued)

Located right off of Walnut Street, this eclectic restaurant and bar offers half-price food after 10 p.m., and hosts popular local music acts such as This Band is Called the You, School of Athens, and Idiosympathy. Nestled in yuppy Shadyside, the Deli is the closest thing to a hipster bar that Walnut Street can speak of.

Shady Grove
5500 Walnut St., Shadyside
(412) 697-0909

This Shadyside hotspot is known for its trendy New York-style décor, and a busy (and often loud) atmosphere. Many students come here for beer specials, as well as frozen margaritas and daiquiris. Right upstairs is the site of the Walnut Grill, a nice spot to dine with friends before drinking the night away.

Student Favorites:
Hemingway's Café
Peter's Pub
Mad Mex
Margarita Mama's
Matrix

Primary Areas with Nightlife:
Oakland
Shadyside
South Side
Station Square
the Strip

Cheapest Place to Get a Drink:
Hemingway's Café

Local Specialties:
Iron City and I.C. Light

Other Places to Check Out:
Bar 11, Bar Louie, Bootlegger's, Casey's, Club Café, Club Havana, Doc's, Jack's, Jekyll And Hyde's, Mario's, Pittsburgh Café, Smokin' Joe's, Tiki Lounge, Touch, William Penn Tavern, The World

Favorite Drinking Games:
Beer Pong
Card Games
Power Hour

Bars Close At:
1:40 a.m.–2 a.m.

Useful Resources for Nightlife
www.barsmart.com
www.pghnightlife.com
www.pghcitypaper.com

What to Do if You're Not 21
There are usually house parties going on in South Oakland over the weekends, and oftentimes, a Pitt or CMU frat is hosting some sort of event. There is always bowling, movies, and shopping open to students; Oakland, South Side, Squirrel Hill, and Shadyside boast their own small cultural districts, complete with coffee shops like Shadyside/East Liberty's Quiet Storm and South Side's Beehive, and tons of restaurants that are popular. Schenley Park is right near campus, with a lot of outdoor area for walking, biking, or just hanging out.

Did You Know?
Telefact, a student-run campus group, sponsors and staffs a hotline that students can call for information during the week. By calling (412) 624-FACT between 12 p.m. and 5 p.m. on weekdays, you can talk to a **student operator who will answer questions about local events, movie times, bus schedules**, and much more! For more information on this great service, check out: *www.pitt.edu/~telefact*.

As an attempt to connect Pitt students to Pittsburgh's art scene, the school offers a **student-only program called Pitt Arts**, in which the University buys tickets for plays, visiting speakers, art exhibits, dance performances, musicals, or other cool events in the Pittsburgh area, as well as those traveling events passing though the city, and offers them to students either for free, or at very low cost. Tickets are divied out on a first-come, first-serve basis, so as soon as a student hears about a coming attraction, they need to check out Pitt Art's Web site at *www.pitt.edu/~pittarts* to reserve their spots.

The College Prowler Take On...
Greek Life

Greek life is definitely visible on campus, and students are aware of its presence. It does not, however, dominate the social scene in any way. Many students who choose to go Greek do so under little or no pressure. There are plenty of Greek organizations to join on campus, and each is different and unique in its own way—there's a lot of time to get to know them before deciding to pledge. Overall, the Greek community accounts for a very small percentage of students. Joining will obviously earn you some new friends and resources for entertainment and leadership; choosing not to join, though, shouldn't have any effect on you at all. Many who are involved in the fraternities and sororities feel that Greek life is a rewarding opportunity, and have no regrets.

For those who don't go Greek, many find they can still hang out with Greek friends, or attend functions and parties. It will be a little more difficult to get into parties if you're a guy, but with all the house parties in the area, this shouldn't be too much of a problem. In everyday life, the Greek system is seen as just another part of campus, and there's little to no tension between Greeks and non-Greeks.

B-

The College Prowler® Grade on
Greek Life: B-

A high grade in Greek Life indicates that sororities and fraternities are not only present, but also active on campus. Other determining factors include the variety of houses available and the respect the Greek community receives from the rest of the campus.

Students Speak Out On...
Nightlife

> "I really haven't been to many of the bars or clubs. We have a couple around campus—most of them are strict, but some aren't. It sort of depends. There are bars and clubs in downtown Pittsburgh that are pretty easy to get to if you're underage."

"In Pittsburgh, there is a good strip of bars. Mario's in South Side is pretty good, although there are a lot more. My friends who go to the bars in Pittsburgh always meet up and go around from place to place. As far as clubs go, **The Upstage is a great Oakland club.** I'm not 100 percent sure what type of music they play there now. I think it's often techno or dance."

"Starting with bars around campus, Peter's is a great place for listening to good music, playing some darts, and being surrounded by Greeks. Hemingway's is a great place for a more relaxed atmosphere. There's another bar that used to be called Cumpie's, but it's always changing owners and has a new name practically every weekend. **Off campus, there are hundreds of bars and clubs**; this is not an exaggeration. The places to go are on the South Side, the Strip District, or Station Square. The top clubs are Matrix, Margarita Mama's, and Saddle Ridge. Thursday is the night to party."

"Around campus, it's mostly small college bars—always packed, and pretty cheap. Off campus, there is a place called the Strip District, which is basically **a mile-long run of huge clubs**; it's really jumping on weekends. If you have the cash, it is an awesome time."

Q "Bars and clubs are all over the place. The Strip, which is close to Oakland, has **tons of bars where the Steelers go**. You just have to find a way to get in if you're not 21."

Q "There are a lot of bars around campus, and **the good clubs are at the Strip**, which is about a 20-minute bus ride."

Q "There are lots of bars, but I'm under 21, so I don't know many. I basically know the clubs that have concerts. The Upstage is a good one, depending on your musical taste, and it's **about a block from the freshman dorms**. I've seen a bunch of shows there, but there aren't as many now—it used to be called 'Club Laga,' and it was a bigger venue for bands then. One of the bands I saw there was Dashboard Confessional."

Q "There are tons of clubs, bars, and restaurants off campus; Oakland is **right in the center of it all**. If you go to the South Side, Carson Street is nothing but clubs and bars. Make sure you have a good fake ID."

Q "The bars and clubs in the area are lots of fun. **Mad Mex has great margaritas**. Off campus, two fun areas are the Strip District, where there are lots of clubs, and South Side, which has lots of fun bars."

Q "Parties are fun, but don't get yourself in trouble. Bars in Pittsburgh can't be beat. **Clubs leave a little to be desired**, but if you're dying for a night of dancing, try the Strip District."

Q "Most of the clubs are in the Strip District—they're all cool. I've only been to two, only because I'm cheap, and they're kind of expensive. **Bars are everywhere in Pittsburgh**. There are plenty around campus, and there are many more on the South Side—I mean a whole lot."

Q "The clubs are usually overcrowded with trashy people, but once in a while, you can find a decent place. The bars, on the other hand, usually have **great happy hour/drink specials, decent music, good atmosphere**, and you can come casual or decked out and still fit in. Try the Southside, Station Square, or the Waterfront for some fun bars!"

Q "I don't remember what house parties are like anymore! They were pretty easy to spot when I was a freshman, but I've heard that has changed. As for bars and clubs. I'm not 21 yet, but I know that **there is a large assortment of bars**—some of the favorites being Peter's Pub, Hemingway's, and Bootlegger's. There are a lot of clubs downtown."

The College Prowler Take On...
Nightlife

There are plenty of things going on in Pittsburgh any given night, and generally, as long as you're willing to seek out activities, you won't be at a loss. There are a number of bars close to campus that are popular with Pitt students, and even more up the street in Shadyside that are usually frequented by the CMU and med-school crowd. If you're willing to hop a bus, the bars of downtown and the clubs of the Strip District and Station Square all open up as potential hangouts, and these areas get very crowded around weekends. Many students choose to stick around Oakland, for the most part—the drink specials and convenience can't be beat, and by the end of your 21st year, you'll probably know a lot of people in the local bar scene. Parties run rampant around campus on weekends, between South Oakland and CMU house parties, and the frat events at both schools. Guys will have a hard time getting into the frats, but girls shouldn't have any trouble. House parties, on the other hand, are open to everyone.

With the recent closing of Club Laga and Rosebud, a void has opened up in the music scene that nothing has really filled. "The World," a new venue in the Strip, is one effort to fix that; it hasn't been open long enough to tell if it will be successful, however. Laga provided a great deal of under-21 entertainment that simply isn't available anywhere else. Overall, however, there is still quite a bit to be found around Pitt, no matter how old you are—as long as you're willing to look around and be creative. The city's nightlife shouldn't exhaust itself before the school year does.

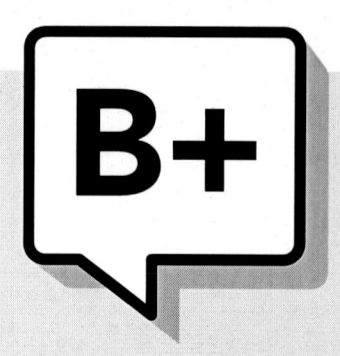

B+

The College Prowler® Grade on
Nightlife: B+

A high grade in Nightlife indicates that there are many bars and clubs in the area that are easily accessible and affordable. Other determining factors include the number of options for the under-21 crowd and the prevalence of house parties.

Greek Life

The Lowdown On...
Greek Life

Number of Fraternities:
17

Number of Sororities:
11

Undergrad Men in Fraternities:
8%

Undergrad Women in Sororities:
7%

Fraternities:
Alpha Epsilon Pi
Delta Chi
Delta Phi
Delta Tau Delta
Kappa Sigma
Lamda Chi Alpha
Phi Kappa Theta
Phi Sigma Kappa
Pi Kappa Alpha
Pi Kappa Phi
Sigma Alpha Epsilon
Sigma Alpha Mu
Sigma Chi
Sigma Phi Epsilon
Tau Epsilon Phi
Tau Kappa Epsilon
Zeta Beta Tau

Sororities:
Alpha Delta Pi
Alpha Epsilon Phi
Chi Omega
Delta Delta Delta
Delta Zeta
Delta Phi Epsilon
Kappa Delta
Kappa Kappa Gamma
Sigma Delta Tau
Sigma Sigma Sigma
Theta Phi Alpha

Other Greek Organizations:
Interfraternity Council
National Panhellenic Council
Panhellenic Council

Did You Know?

Greek Week is the most popular Greek event, and it inspires a lot of competition between sororities and fraternities.

Students Speak Out On...
Greek Life

> "There are frats and sororities, but I wasn't in them, and I didn't see too many problems due to them. Frats here are kind of weak from my experience. They're just for freshmen. They get old the older you get."

Q "I am in a sorority, but I didn't join one my first year because I didn't think I wanted to be in one. It's not a big part of campus life, though, **once you are in one you notice it a lot more than when you weren't**. There are special events for Greeks that are held to raise money, but basically, it's not really a big part of life here."

Q "Greek life at Pitt is really great. I have been part of Greek life since my freshman year, and I think it has only helped me to meet more people, and get more involved. Plus, there are so many benefits, like networking for jobs in the future with alumni, or getting advice on classes and profs from your brothers or sisters. There are **always a lot of fun events to participate in**, and Greek Week is a blast."

Q "After hearing about an annual frat party where fish are hung in bags and eaten alive for laughs, **I boycotted Greek life at Pitt**."

Q "I'm not in a frat—**I'm just not into the whole thing**, but I go up to the houses occasionally, and it's not a bad time. Frats are pretty big on campus, but not huge—you do not have to be in one to have a social life."

Q "I'm not familiar with the Greek life; **it doesn't seem to dominate my social scene**, but that's entirely subjective."

Q "Frat parties are pretty much every weekend. The frats are located in upper campus, and the sororities are all in one dorm near the rest of the dorms. **I wouldn't say they dominate the social scene**. They are there if you want to participate. If you don't, you can still go to the frat parties."

Q "Fraternities are not that big on campus, so **they don't dominate campus life** like at other big schools. They do their fundraisers, elections, and have parties, but besides that, I don't pay attention to them."

Q "Going Greek has been great for me. One of the most important things about it is that you are having all this fun, but you also help out the community. **A lot of the Greek events are fundraisers** to benefit a different non-profit each year, and it's also a good way to become a leader on campus. Greek life doesn't consume Pitt's campus, but it's big enough to be worth it if that's what you're interested in."

Q "When you arrive on campus as a freshman, the Greek scene is something that everyone gets a taste of. You'll go party with them and maybe even pledge, but there's no pressure to join, and pretty much anyone can get into any frat party, as long as they know someone. **Frats throw decent parties after major Pitt sporting events**, but besides that, they're pretty corny"

Q "Greek life is not big at Pitt at all. There's so much other stuff to do off campus, from partying to clubbing and bar hopping. If you are really into the whole frat thing, then it's a great experience. You will probably develop long-lasting friendships and **a sense of family on campus**. But you do not need a frat or sorority to feel at home on campus."

Q "On such a large, diverse campus, **Greek life is regarded as more of yet another student option**, rather than a popularity or recreation must."

Q "The Greeks have **something going on almost every weekend**. It does not necessarily dominate the social scene, but if Greek life is your thing, there is always something going on."

Q "Greek life—take it or leave it. It's all up to you. Greek life does not dominate Pitt's social scene. **You can have a wonderful time being Greek**; you can also have a wonderful time by making friends other places."

Q "The Greek life at Pitt is good because if you want to be Greek, you have ample opportunity, and **the Greeks do a lot of good things on campus**. However, if that isn't your cup of tea, you can remain active on campus through the other 300 organizations."

Drug Scene

The Lowdown On...
Drug Scene

Most Prevalent Drugs on Campus:
Alcohol
Ecstasy
Marijuana

Liquor-Related Referrals:
6

Liquor-Related Arrests:
199

Drug-Related Referrals:
15

Drug-Related Arrests:
44

Drug Counseling Programs

Group counseling sessions, as well as individual meetings, about drug or alcohol concerns are held through the University Counseling Center. In addition, information and classes about drugs and alcohol are available through Student Health Services.

University Counseling Center

334 William Pitt Union
(412) 648-7930
www.counseling.pitt.edu
counsel@pitt.edu

Student Health Services

Suite 500,
Medical Arts Building
3708 Fifth Avenue
(412) 383-1800
www.studhlth.pitt.edu
studhlth@pitt.edu

Students Speak Out On...
Drug Scene

> "I would say the drug scene is probably on average with most other schools. It exists if you want it to, but you can completely avoid it if you prefer."

Q "I really can't say, because I don't ever buy, and I rarely do anything. **I just stick to drinking and occasionally weed**, but I never buy or know where to. I know a ton of people who do, though, so I'm guessing there is a pretty big drug scene."

Q "It's not to the point that police are needed, but **some people have their hands on drugs**."

Q "Drugs exist here, and there are many more users than I think there would be at most other schools. It's not prevalent if you don't want it to be. Most of my friends don't do drugs, and while I occasionally do, it's not something that is widespread among students. There are **definitely no hard drugs here**, though. I have never seen or even heard of anyone doing cocaine, heroin, or anything of that sort. It's mostly recreational."

Q "Pittsburgh is a city like any other, so **I imagine it isn't hard to get a hold of drugs**. However, you can choose your own friends, so if you don't want to hear about it, you won't."

Q "I haven't seen any drugs on campus, or at any parties. I can say, however, that if you want to do some, there are certain people who are known for doing certain things, and **you will find them if you look hard**."

Q "There doesn't seem to be much of a drug problem around campus. Although you can definitely get anything you want, **you rarely hear about more than pot and booze** in the mainstream."

Q "I come from a place where heroin and coke are very common, but on campus, they're unheard of. **Weed is pretty common, and maybe 'E' and acid**, but that's about it. You don't see junkies lying in the gutters or anything. The police have a zero-tolerance policy for drugs, as they do for underage drinking. I never, ever hear of anyone getting caught for drugs, though."

Q "Realistically, **there is a decent-sized drug scene on campus**. I wouldn't go so far as to say that it's becoming a huge problem, and it doesn't seem like it's more prevalent here compared to any other university or college. However, I know if I ever wanted to get drugs, I would know who to get it from. It's all in who you're friends with, and which crowd you're in, I guess."

Q "There is not a big-time drug scene on our campus. Most people are into drinking, though. **You might see weed here and there**, at certain parties, or maybe even in a nightclub, but it's not as common as it is in other places."

Q "Pitt is like everywhere else—**there is drug use**, and the campus police, along with resident assistants, try to crack down on it as much as they can, but they can't be everywhere."

Q "**I'm not into drugs**, but there's always a way to find what you're looking for."

Q "I have never felt pressured into doing anything I didn't want to. That's something I didn't expect when I got here. **I thought college was the place for experimentation**, but honestly, I haven't done much experimenting with substances here besides weed or alcohol. I am completely comfortable with that, too."

Q "I'm going to be 100 percent honest here and say that I know nothing of the drug scene on campus. I've never tried to get involved, so **I don't know if it's readily available** or something to be concerned about."

Q "Alcohol, pot, and occasionally some ecstasy or the like are what you're going to find around campus. **The city is apparently known for its heroin**, but you don't see that at Pitt. Overall, it's a very underground, safe scene—definitely easy enough to avoid, if that's what you want."

The College Prowler Take On...
Drug Scene

Drugs exist on any college campus, and Pitt is about on par with other large public schools as far as prevalence goes. If you're in a position to see the drug scene at all, most of what you'll encounter will be alcohol and marijuana. Ecstasy, acid, and occasionally other "hard" drugs may appear, but use of these is even more subdued than marijuana. Although most of the common hard drugs can be found somewhere in the city of Pittsburgh, they've largely stayed outside of campus and away from Pitt students. All drug use around campus is discreet; many students have never personally encountered the drug scene at all, or they have only seen it from a distance at parties. You shouldn't need to worry about any pressure to use drugs, as long as you're careful about whom you make friends with. A good bit of the University's social scene includes, or revolves around, alcohol, and all but the most anti-social underclassmen are bound to encounter it at some point.

Even so, there still isn't a great deal of pressure to drink—again, this depends a lot on where you spend your time and how you choose your friends. It's important to remember that, for all the drunken parties you can find each weekend, there are also plenty of student group events and other things going on, both on and off campus, that don't involve alcohol at all. The decision to drink is left to you.

B-

The College Prowler® Grade on
Drug Scene: B-

A high grade in the Drug Scene indicates that drugs are not a noticeable part of campus life; drug use is not visible, and no pressure to use them seems to exist.

Campus Strictness

The Lowdown On...
Campus Strictness

What Are You Most Likely to Get Caught Doing on Campus?
- Drinking underage
- Public urination or indecency
- Parking illegally
- Keeping a George Foreman Grill in your room
- Blasting your speakers too loudly into the Quad

Students Speak Out On...
Campus Strictness

> "The campus police are real police officers, and have to uphold the law, but everything they do is in the best interest of the student. They are not overzealous, and don't look to pick on people."

Q "They are pretty strict if you get caught with drugs or alcohol. They just started a new thing where **they call your parents to let them know** that you have been caught. As long as you don't do it in the dorms, you probably won't get caught. Most parties don't get busted unless they are out of control."

Q "**In the dorms, it's strict**. In the apartments, if there is a resident assistant, it's kind of strict, but not bad. There are ways around everything, though. The nicest places to live on campus are in Bouquet Gardens. Drinking and anything else in those places is easy to do, and almost risk-free, as far as cops go."

Q "**The cops that walk around are nice**. I can't say it for all of them, but most of them don't care if you're drinking or even 'smoking' as long as you aren't causing problems—that has been said to me by a couple of cops who I've talked to."

Q "As far as I know, I think **the campus police don't really play around with drug use**. Drinking, on the other hand, is something I've never gotten caught for. I think, unless you're acting crazy, you're not going to get caught drinking."

Q "It's not like the cops are unaware that underage drinking goes on. Just **don't be running around drunk all over the streets**, and you're fine."

Q "They claim to be strict, but **we have plenty of fun**, nonetheless. I don't know many people who get caught."

Q "The cops usually don't bother you too much. Don't keep any alcohol in your dorm, or your RA might find it, and you'll get a nice fine. Drugs are easier to hide, but I don't suggest having them. You have to be a complete moron to get caught for underage drinking. Pretty much as long as you're in a privately-owned building, you can't get busted. **The cops never check the frats**, either."

Q "The whole police strictness thing is kind of a hot topic right now. I was never once caught when I was underage, and I went to a lot of house parties. It's easy to tell when someone is having a party. **Most of the time, the police just ignore it, unless a neighbor complains**. Then they go to the door and give a warning, but sometimes they'll come back, bust the party, and tell everyone to go home. That only happened to me three times in three years. At other schools, they take your name as you walk out the door, but I've heard of that happening here only once."

Q "If they catch you drinking, or with alcohol on campus, you're screwed. **You get cited, have to take a drug and alcohol class, and sometimes have to pay a fine**. If it's on campus, you go on probation for two years. If you don't screw up in that time period, it gets erased from your record. Sometimes they'll cite people who have been brought into the emergency room after blacking out, which is really messed up."

Q "If you have half a brain, use it, and **avoid drinking or using drugs in the dorms**, or around police-sensitive areas. Don't come back to the dorm too drunk to pull yourself together, or too high to remember which dorm room you live in."

Q "Whatever you do, be careful when it comes to screwing around. I know people that have been caught for underage drinking, and it is a big hassle paying fines and taking classes. When it comes to drugs, **your days at Pitt could be numbered if you get caught**. Don't jeopardize your college experience over something stupid."

Q "The police patrol the streets on the weekend, but they won't stop you unless you are noticeably intoxicated. I think **they have been stricter about parties recently**, but that's only hearsay."

Q "The security guards will call the campus police if they think you're a threat to yourself. **If the cops catch you, you'll have a fine**, classes, a judicial board hearing, and quite possibly worse."

Q "The Pitt police are incredibly annoying about kids on campus who drink, and you'll always see **students in the *Pitt News* Police Blotter getting under-ages**. It's such a pain, because they're always on everyone's case, but if you're smart about it, you won't get caught. Usually they're not too bad with parties—they only send people home if it gets really out of control."

The College Prowler Take On...
Campus Strictness

How you perceive Pitt's campus strictness is very dependent on what you're caught doing, where you're doing it, and who catches you. In general, campus police and resident assistants are very strict when it comes to drug and alcohol use. On campus, resident assistants are slightly more lenient with their dorm floors regarding alcohol use; though, this doesn't mean you should try to get away with underage drinking in the dorms. Drug use is even more dangerous, and both campus police and University staff are quick to crack down on drug violations. Punishment for getting caught with drugs or alcohol means a fine, a notification sent to your parents, and a required class in substance abuse. All of these things are completely avoidable, however, if you're mature enough about what you're doing. Most arrests and citations are the result of students being loud and rowdy, or otherwise drawing attention to themselves. Off-campus parties are rarely busted. When they are, those who live in the busted apartment or house have a lot of trouble on their hands. In the houses around campus, it's probably going to be campus police who break up the party. You'll still be subject to University discipline if you're caught, though, and there's a good chance that those who don't live at the apartment/house will just be told to leave.

City police are the most lenient of all the authorities you'll encounter because they have more important things to worry about than dealing with drunken college kids. They won't often show up to parties unless a formal complaint has been issued. Clearly, the key is to know your limits and not make a spectacle of yourself; most of the students who find themselves in trouble with the Pitt police have done something to ask for it.

B

The College Prowler® Grade on Campus Strictness: B

A high Campus Strictness grade implies an overall lenient atmosphere; police and RAs are fairly tolerant, and the administration's rules are flexible.

Parking

The Lowdown On...
Parking

Parking Permits:
Indoor garages $92 per month

Outdoor lots $85 per month

Evening permits $62 per semester

Motorcycle permits $25 per semester

Student Parking Lot?
Yes

Freshmen Allowed to Park?
Yes

Common Parking Tickets:
Parking without a permit: $25

No parking zone: $25

Handicapped zone: $100

Parking Services Office

204 Brackenridge Hall

(412) 624-4034

www.pts.pitt.edu

parking@bc.pitt.edu

Permits at Pitt are assigned by area—your permit will be for a specific garage or lot; rates listed describe different types of lots that are available. In the event that you can't park in your assigned lot/garage (i.e.: the lot is full, blocked by snow), your permit will be temporarily validated in the Soldiers and Sailors or O'Hara garages.

Did You Know?

Best Places to Find a Parking Spot
- Metered lots
- Soldiers and Sailors garage

Good Luck Getting a Parking Spot Here!
- Forbes Avenue or Fifth Avenue
- Schenley Quad

If you need to make a quick stop at a campus building but **don't have the permit for its lot, just leave your flashers on**! With a valid parking permit displayed and your four-way flashers activated, you're allowed to park for up to 15 minutes in any lot.

Need a jump start? Locked your keys in your car? Call MAP, **Pitt's Motorist Assistant Program**, at (412) 624-4034.

Students Speak Out On...
Parking

> "Parking on campus is hard to get because it's in the middle of a city. Your best bet is to pay for a permit early, or get a lease at a garage."

Q "Apparently, there is enough space to park on campus. Pitt has at least one permit garage for students who want to keep cars, but parking permits are still very expensive. Outside of the permit parking, you have to take your chances with Oakland street parking, which is often very hard to get. **Keeping a car really isn't necessary** for getting around the city, and is expensive enough that I'd recommend catching buses or mooching rides from other people while you live in the dorms."

Q "If you have a parking permit, there is no problem parking. If you don't, **parking is horrible**."

Q "Parking is awful. Even if you get a parking space from the school, it'll probably be way up on a hill in the parking garage, and it's a pain to use. **Parking on the streets is even worse**. There are never any spots, and you have to keep feeding the meters."

Q "**Parking is expensive at Pitt**. I don't have a car out here, so I don't know a lot about it."

Q "Parking in Oakland is terrible for students, and people coming to visit, because there never is any, and no one ever has quarters. **Parking for students is usually in the OC lot**, which is on upper campus at the top of Cardiac Hill (which means you're going to have to walk pretty far, or take a shuttle to get to your car)."

Q "Wow . . . parking is insane! Always keep tons of quarters on hand in the event that you can find a space, or park in a nearby store lot or non-permit area, and take the bus into Oakland. **Campus parking permits aren't guaranteed**; I had a friend who was forced to give up her space in a lot when there was a home basketball game, and she had to pay to park her car until the game was over."

Q "The bus system pretty much substitutes for any car. You really don't need to go any place the bus can't take you, and **having a car in the city is just a huge liability**."

Q "I haven't had any trouble finding parking spaces near my apartment. The closer you get to campus, the harder it is, but **it's pretty cheap as long as you park on the street**."

Q "Parking is awful. We are in the middle of the city, and most students who park have their own apartments or relatives that live nearby. **You can rent spaces in local garages for about $80 per month** indoors, or $65 per month outdoors. We also have three big parking garages, which are open from 6 a.m. to 1 a.m. every day."

Q "Parking is **one of the bad things at Pitt**; there is not much because it's in the city."

Q "Parking sucks. It costs a fortune to park on campus, and parking off campus is just as terrible. It's so bad because of the UPMC hospital employees—**they take all the spaces and fill the garages**."

Q "**If you have a car here, good luck finding parking**. There is no way you will be able to find a spot consistently if you commute to campus with a car. If you get a garage space, then you will be fine. I do suggest having a car, though, after your freshman year. It's useful when you want to go to the mall, the movies, or just leave town for a road trip."

Q "Don't bring a car until you move off campus. You don't need it. Everything you need is either in walking distance or a short bus ride away. **It's insanely expensive to park on campus**, and there's not really anywhere you can leave your car off campus."

Q "**I wouldn't suggest bringing a car** to campus if you are living on campus. The parking can be a little expensive and inconvenient, and is generally not needed due to the bus system."

The College Prowler Take On...
Parking

The University of Pittsburgh is one of the few schools that allows freshmen to bring cars. Most students who do bring cars are given parking passes for the OC lot—the area on upper campus near the athletic facilities. While this is a lower-traffic area, and it can be nice to avoid the congestion of central Oakland, the OC can be quite a hike. Unless you're living in Sutherland Hall, Pennsylvania Hall, or one of the frat houses, you're going to have to climb "Cardiac Hill" whenever you want to get to your car. The cost of permits doesn't justify this walk for many students, and it definitely detracts from the convenience of having a car. By 5 p.m. weeknights, and all day on weekends, most of the lots on campus open up to anyone with a permit. That is, you don't have to stick to the OC, or wherever you've been assigned, if you don't have a permit; though, you're still stuck with street parking or public garages. Metered parking is free after 6 p.m., but this is too late to matter for most students who try to drive to campus. Parking in Pittsburgh isn't convenient at all—the streets tend to be small and crowded, and it's difficult to be sure where you can safely leave your car. If you have an off-campus house or apartment, it's a good idea to make sure there will be adequate parking before you sign your lease.

Overall, the cost and inconvenience of parking at Pitt makes it too much to bother with for most students. Public transportation is free, and buses will take you almost everywhere you'll need to go. While a car can be a great boon for escaping city limits on weekends, you have to weigh how much you're actually going to do this against the effort of keeping a vehicle around. You'll probably find that, for daily activities, a car is more trouble than it's worth.

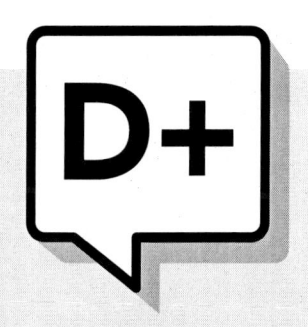

D+

The College Prowler® Grade on
Parking: D+

A high grade in this section indicates that parking is both available and affordable, and that parking enforcement isn't overly severe.

Transportation

The Lowdown On...
Transportation

Ways to Get Around Town:

On Campus

Department of Parking, Transportation, and Services
Forbes Pavilion
3525 Forbes Ave.
www.pc.pitt.edu/transportation

Pitt's Transportation Services runs the on-campus shuttles, as well as the SafeRider program and shuttles for students with disabilities.

In addition, this office manages a limited number of buses home for holiday and University breaks.

Public Transportation

Port Authority of
Allegheny County
345 Sixth Ave., 3rd Floor
(412) 442-2000
www.ridegold.com

The Port Authority is responsible for public transportation around Allegheny County. Routes include all Port Authority Transit (PAT) buses, as well as The 'T' (a half subway, half tram rail line), and the Allegheny and Monongahela inclines.

Taxi Cabs

Checker Cab
(412) 381-5600

Yellow Cab Co.
(412) 321-8100

Car Rentals

Alamo
local: (412) 472-5060
national: (800) 327-9633
www.alamo.com

Avis
local: (412) 472-5200
national: (800) 831-2847
www.avis.com

Budget
local: (412) 472-5252
national: (800) 527-0700
www.budget.com

Dollar
local: (412) 472-5100
national: (800) 800-4000
www.dollar.com

Enterprise
local: (412) 472-3490
national: (800) 736-8222
www.enterprise.com

(Car Rentals, continued)

Hertz
local: (412) 472-5955
national: (800) 654-3131
www.hertz.com

National
local: (412) 472-5094
national: (800) 227-7368
www.nationalcar.com

Best Ways to Get Around Town

Bicycle
PAT buses
Walking

Ways to Get Out of Town:

Airlines Serving Pittsburgh

American Airlines
(800) 433-7300
www.aa.com

Continental
(800) 523-3273
www.continental.com

Delta
(800) 221-1212
www.delta.com

Northwest
(800) 225-2525
www.nwa.com

Southwest
(800) 435-9792
www.southwest.com

TWA
(800) 221-2000
www.twa.com

United
(800) 241-6522
www.united.com

(Airlines Serving Pittsburgh, continued)
US Airways
(800) 428-4322
www.usairways.com

Airport
Pittsburgh International Airport
(412) 472-3525
www.pitairport.com
info@flypittsburgh.com
The Pittsburgh International Airport is 22 miles and approximately 30 minutes driving time from Pitt.

How to Get to the Airport
Airlines Transportation Company Inc.
(412) 471-8900

Airport Flyer
PAT's 28X Shuttle. The bus has numerous stops throughout campus, and the trip takes about 40 minutes; as with all PAT buses, the 28X is free with your student ID.

A cab ride to the airport costs about $35.

Greyhound
Pittsburgh Greyhound Trailways Bus Terminal
11th St. & Liberty Ave.
Pittsburgh, PA 15222
(412) 392-6513
www.greyhound.com
The Greyhound bus terminal is located in downtown Pittsburgh, approximately four miles from campus.
For schedule information visit their Web site, or call (800) 231-2222.

Amtrak
Pittsburgh Amtrak Train Station
1100 Liberty Ave.
Pittsburgh, PA 15222
(412) 471-6172
www.amtrak.com
The Amtrak station is located in downtown Pittsburgh, approximately four miles from campus. For schedule information visit their Web site, or call (800) 872-7245.

Travel Agents
Council Travel
118 Meyran Ave., Oakland
(412) 683-1881

Students Speak Out On...
Transportation

> "Public transportation is reliable to get you pretty much anywhere around Pittsburgh. And the best part about it is that it is all free!"

Q "Public transportation is very convenient. **We can ride buses all over Allegheny County for free** with our Pitt IDs, and the University also has its own set of buses and shuttles to take students to points all over campus."

Q "Everyone uses the bus system. **If you have a Pitt ID, you ride for free**. You can go anywhere, all over the city."

Q "For the most part, buses can take you wherever you need to go in Pittsburgh, and they provide a good opportunity to explore the city. Over the last few years, the **bus schedule has been getting cut back progressively**, to the point where nothing runs after 1 a.m. on weekdays and 3 a.m. on weekends. As long as you don't want to go far late at night, you should have no problems getting along without a car."

Q "Buses are free for students, and they are always around. **Routes take you right downtown**, and to anywhere else you would want to go."

Q "If you are a Pitt student, you can ride all the buses for free. The same goes for the subway, called the 'T,' though, it isn't much. You can **also ride Pittsburgh's multiple inclines, which are beautiful**."

Q "Public transportation is great. There are **lots of buses, and they come by frequently**, though, you might have to wait awhile late at night. There is always a way to get anywhere and everywhere, so even if you live a few neighborhoods away (which is sometimes cheaper), you can always get to school."

Q "Transportation is really good. **We have buses running all the time**, and they can take you anywhere you want to go."

Q "**Weekday public transportation is very reliable**, efficient, and most of all, free with your Pitt ID. Weekend and holiday transportation is still free, but very infrequent."

Q "You definitely don't need a car. The buses are free, and **the whole bus system is awesome**. There are buses everywhere. You never have to wait more than 10 or 15 minutes for a bus during the day. I have a car here, but it's only because I love it, and so I can drive home whenever I want to—if you go anywhere in the city, public transportation is the way to go!"

Q "It's great. **A ton of buses come every few minutes**, and if you have your Pitt ID, you get free transportation for about five to six years."

Q "You can ride the PAT buses for free with your Pitt ID. Buses go almost anywhere in the city you would be interested in and, **for the most part, they are clean and pleasant**."

Q "There are public bus stops all around campus, which we have access to for free. Also, **there is a campus shuttle**. Both run on a regular basis."

Q "There are bus stops all over campus. They can drop you off downtown, in Squirrel Hill, Shadyside, Monroeville at the mall, South Hills for the bars, or on the Waterfront pretty easily. **Pay attention to when the last buses run** so you don't get stuck somewhere!"

Q "The public transportation is great. There are always buses running to every part of Pittsburgh imaginable. The only drawback is that it takes a while to get to farther locations because of all the stops that they make. On the upside, **your Pitt ID gets you onto all of the public forms of transportation for free**, and all of it runs right through campus. Watch out for the bus lane on Fifth Avenue, though—it runs opposite of the one-way traffic, and they won't stop for you, they'll just beep!"

The College Prowler Take On...
Transportation

Free public transportation is one of the biggest perks of being an ID-carrying Pitt student. Both the city bus lines and the 'T' are free, and can give you access to the expansive Pittsburgh neighborhoods served by their routes. Local shopping districts and areas with nightlife are close by, and if you're willing to ride a bit farther, you can reach a few different shopping plazas, as well as the Homestead Waterfront, (which boasts a Target, a Best Buy, restaurants, and a huge movie theatre, among others). Free bus rides are especially great for going places like downtown, where parking is always a hassle; most of the buses that come through Oakland go downtown, so there's never much of a wait.

The biggest complaint about public transit is availability. During the daytime, you shouldn't have any problem getting where you need to go—buses to all major areas run frequently, especially during rush hour, and all routes are active. At night, however, options tend to be more limited. Some bus routes quit running around midnight on weeknights, and none go past 3 a.m.; on weekends, it's a little better, but you'll still want to check schedules carefully before you go too far out. Some routes only run once an hour after peak times, and that can seem like forever in the chilly Pittsburgh winter. Despite this drawback, however, the buses are too convenient to pass up—if you explore the quirks of each route early in your college career, you'll not only learn the city, but also be able to get places faster and with less trouble.

B+

The College Prowler® Grade on
Transportation: B+

A high grade for Transportation indicates that campus buses, public buses, cabs, and rental cars are readily-available and affordable. Other determining factors include proximity to an airport and the necessity of transportation.

Weather

The Lowdown On...
Weather

Average Temperature:
Fall: 53 °F
Winter: 30 °F
Spring: 50 °F
Summer: 71 °F

Average Precipitation:
Fall: 2.83 in.
Winter: 2.64 in.
Spring: 3.33 in.
Summer: 3.82 in.

Students Speak Out On...
Weather

> "We see all four seasons. It's warm and rainy in the spring, hot in the summer, cooler in the fall, and snowy or slushy in the winter."

Q "The **weather is very unpredictable**. I grew up in New Jersey, so I guess I'm used to the Northeast, but I like it."

Q "**Bring a raincoat**! Pittsburgh weather is the strangest in the entire country. Over the past few weeks, one day it was 32 degrees, the next day it was 78 and rainy, the next day it was 45 degrees, and then the next day it was 82 and humid. You can never predict our weather."

Q "The weather tends to be alright. It doesn't really snow that much during the winter, at least not since I have been going here, but **the dirty slush never seems to go away**, and you get tired of that pretty quickly. It actually rains more than it snows, so bring an umbrella."

Q "Pittsburgh winters are very cold, but still a step up from most of PA and the Northeast in general. **Layering is the way to go** in any situation, but warmer clothes are always a safe bet."

Q "It's gray, sometimes with a shed of light, and then gray and rainy again. We don't get the greatest weather. When it does get nice, it's like a holiday, and everyone is out enjoying it. The **Cathedral Lawn is a fabulous spot for sunning, talking, and napping**. I'm used to Pennsylvania weather, but Pittsburgh's is pretty bad, even for us."

Q "The weather is pretty unpredictable. **This past spring was crazy-warm**—we went to the park, and tanned in the middle of April, which isn't normal."

Q "Usually, we have a nice fall. **Winter is very snowy in January**, and spring can either be almost freezing through May, or unusually warm like it was this year."

Q "It is sunny sometimes, which makes campus look nice. When it rains, it looks dreary. **It gets windy and cold in the winter**, but snow doesn't usually accumulate in the city. It is hot in the summer."

Q "Most of the time, it's relatively mild through November, colder during the winter months, then warms up in the middle of April. **Bring plenty of long-sleeved shirts** along with sweats, as the majority of the year takes place during the cooler months."

Q "Never leave the house in Pittsburgh without an umbrella! **The weather is almost always iffy**; it might be beautiful and 80 degrees throughout the day, and then the sky will erupt at 9 p.m. when you're about to go out for the evening."

Q "It's kind of crappy in the winter. It's usually overcast and windy. We haven't gotten that much snow in the three years I've been here. It rains a lot, but **the summer is absolutely gorgeous**."

Q "Your best bet is to bring some of everything, dress in layers, and **bring a sturdy umbrella** because you never know what you're going to get when you come—each year it seems to be totally different."

Q "Pittsburgh is **hot and humid in the summer**, and cold and bitter in the winter. Plan accordingly. For me, that means shorts and T-shirts for the fall, and sweaters, jeans, warm shoes, and a heavy winter coat for the winter."

Q "There are four full seasons in Pittsburgh. Snow falls in winter, and it gets into the upper 80s in the beginning of fall and the end of spring. **Don't forget an umbrella.**"

The College Prowler Take On...
Weather

Pittsburgh has a typical, Northeastern conglomeration of weather—plenty of sunshine, snow, rain, and clouds. Typical summers range from warm to sweltering, depending on whether you're fortunate enough to have air-conditioning. There's always a lot of sun keeping the city warm and bright, and often, humidity runs high. This type of weather usually runs from mid-May until early September, after which it tapers off into winter. During the school year, temperatures often hover around freezing, and effectively keep students from leaving their apartments or dorms, even to go to class. The wind is one of the worst features about Pittsburgh winter; even when it seems like the buildings should act as a windbreak, there are often frigid gusts to deal with when you're out walking.

Students who are not used to this type of weather can have a hard time adjusting to the consecutive dreary days. Overall, however, if you like changing seasons, then you should get along fine in Pittsburgh. Be sure to bring rain gear, and wear clothes that can be layered, and remember that there can be a 30 degree difference between any two days, so it's a good idea to have a wide range of clothing with you when you leave for school.

C-

The College Prowler® Grade on Weather: C-

A high Weather grade designates that temperatures are mild and rarely reach extremes, that the campus tends to be sunny rather than rainy, and that weather is fairly consistent rather than unpredictable.

UNIVERSITY OF PITTSBURGH
Report Card Summary

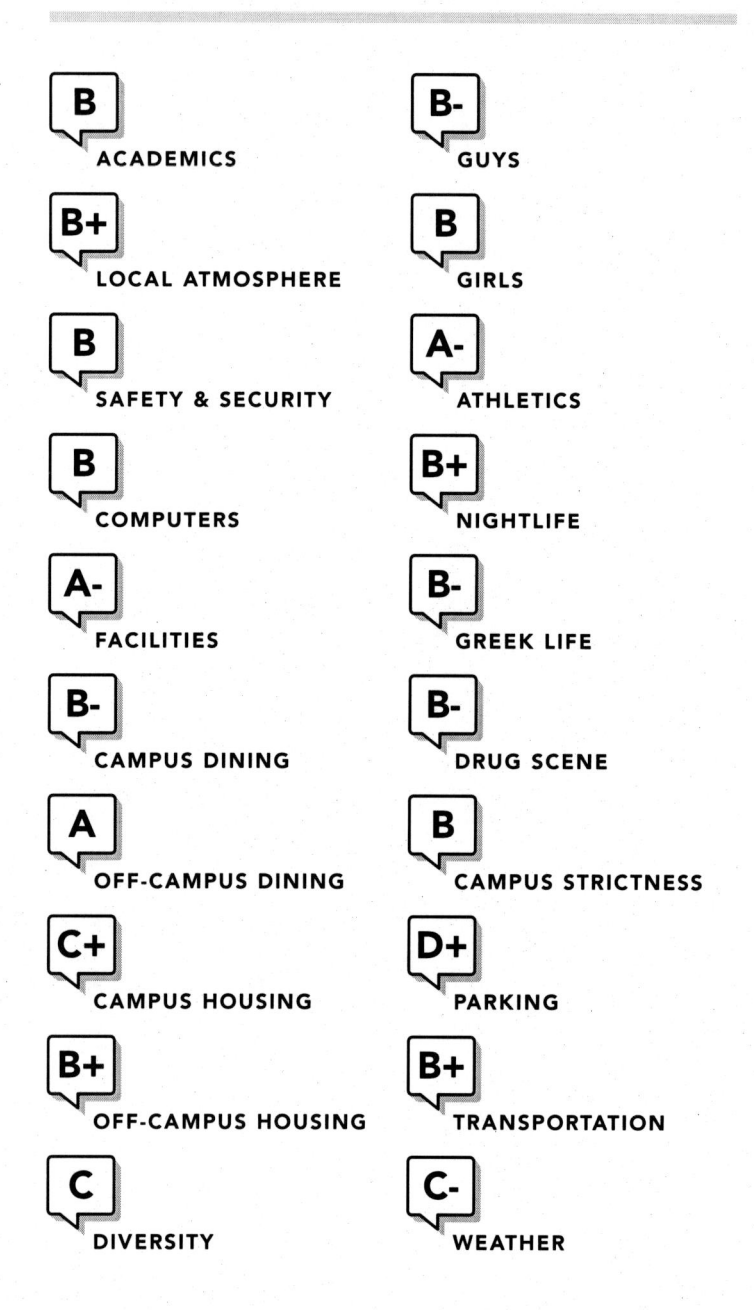

B ACADEMICS

B+ LOCAL ATMOSPHERE

B SAFETY & SECURITY

B COMPUTERS

A- FACILITIES

B- CAMPUS DINING

A OFF-CAMPUS DINING

C+ CAMPUS HOUSING

B+ OFF-CAMPUS HOUSING

C DIVERSITY

B- GUYS

B GIRLS

A- ATHLETICS

B+ NIGHTLIFE

B- GREEK LIFE

B- DRUG SCENE

B CAMPUS STRICTNESS

D+ PARKING

B+ TRANSPORTATION

C- WEATHER

Overall Experience

Students Speak Out On...
Overall Experience

"I love it at Pitt; I wish I was there right now! I know it sounds so corny, but college all goes by so fast."

"Pitt was a great choice. There is enough to do in this city to keep me occupied, and not too much going on so that I stay out of trouble. **The teachers have been helpful and have motivated me** to do better than I have ever done in school before. If Pitt adds a few more academic programs, it will be the perfect school."

"It's been good so far. **Pitt is a school within a city**, but on the downside, there aren't as many different things to do."

Q "I have a great sense of pride in my school—I love the University of Pittsburgh, and I always will. I think it is **an excellent school with a wide range of fields of study** and an immense number of job opportunities in every line of work. No matter what major you choose, you can always walk away with a well-rounded education and great experiences. From partying with friends, to cramming for finals, I wouldn't trade my time at Pitt for the world. Hail to Pitt!"

Q "Overall, **I would do the Pitt experience all over again**. I just graduated and am moving on. I received a very good education, met my fiancé here, made some great friends, always had something to do, and had many opportunities to get involved. I got out of the school what I was willing to put into it."

Q "My overall experience is good, and I cannot say that I wish I were anywhere else. **I transferred here, and I am glad that I did**."

Q "I love it. **I would not go anywhere else**. If you want a diverse campus with lots to do in the surrounding area, pick Pitt."

Q "I like Pitt. The education is good, and **there's fun to be had**. It's not too pricey, either."

Q "Pitt is probably the best choice I've made so far. I went from a 3.4 GPA in high school to a 4.0 in college. **Making the Dean's List is not that hard** if you really try. I would not pick any other college over Pitt."

Q "I've had almost **nothing but positive experiences** at Pitt (except for when West Virginia beat us), and I can't imagine being happier anywhere else."

Q "I love this place. I went through a tough time last year with one of my roommates, and I was going to transfer to Penn State. Then I realized that I was going to miss everyone here, as well as the city itself. **Pittsburgh is a place you either love or hate**—I love it. I'm not going to live here my whole life, but I'm making the most of it now. There's so much to do here—there's so much that I haven't even done, and I've been here three years already."

Q "The only stipulation for Pitt is that you have to want to live in a city. I come from a small town, and I really wanted to live in a city. After I graduate from here, I'll move closer to home and find a job, but **I'm not going to live in a big city again**. I like it, but I don't think it's something I want to do for my entire life."

Q "I looked at a couple schools, including one in Philadelphia, before I chose Pitt. I think that Philadelphia is a dump. I like it, but compared to Pittsburgh, it's gross. Pittsburgh is really clean; my parents and I fell in love with it the first time we were here. **My parents are actually jealous of me**—they want to live here. They visit me all the time just to do things here. They're really happy that I'm here."

Q "I love Pitt. I think it is fantastic. Even though **it has little quirks, and sometimes big glitches**, I love my experience here, and I would never trade it in for another."

Q "Thus far, Pitt has seemed like a decent experience. Academically, the classes are well organized, and campus life is basically what I expected as I came here out of high school. I'm glad that I chose Pitt simply because **I've grown to love Pittsburgh** and wouldn't want to be living anywhere else right now."

The College Prowler Take On...
Overall Experience

Overall, students agree that they wouldn't trade their Pitt experiences for anything else. As with most decisions, however, there are a lot of things to consider. If you don't like living in the city, Pittsburgh may not be the place for you; while it doesn't have the huge feel of New York or Philadelphia, the area is definitely urban. Also, Pitt is a large school—you're in for big lecture classes and a somewhat overwhelming campus during the first year or two, though, everything seems to get smaller after you've been around awhile. Weather can be a concern if you're used to warmer climates, as snow and rain are rules of Pittsburgh winter. This is something you can easily get used to, though, so unless you're a die-hard warm weather fan, you should do fine.

What Pitt does offer is high-caliber academics, plenty of student organizations, and frequent opportunities such as study abroad, cultural activities, and sports, among many others. If you're willing to become active on campus, there's a lot more to Pitt than meets the eye. The University's location can also be a great advantage—Pittsburgh itself is a positive environment for students, especially because the city is dominated by colleges and universities. The social scene is always jumping, locals are friendly, and there's always something to do if you explore a little. The best idea is to visit after you've applied and try to get a feel for the area. You can get the same quality education at Pitt that you find in many smaller, expensive schools and pay less to have a vibrant city right at your doorstep.

The Inside Scoop

The Lowdown On...
The Inside Scoop

Pitt Slang:

Know the slang, know the school. The following is a list of things you really need to know before coming to Pitt. The more of these words you know, the better off you'll be.

The Ashtray – The area outside of Towers; popular for students to smoke and hang out.

Club Hillman – Nickname for Hillman Library.

Hemmie's – Hemingway's Café.

Ho-Land – Nickname for Holland Hall, an all-female residence hall in the Quad.

The "O" – The Original Hot Dog Shop.

Panther Central – The offices in Towers lobby for the ID service and housing/dining.

The Quad – Schenley Quad, where eight of the 11 residence halls are located.

Upper Campus – The area with all the athletic facilities, frats, and newer dorms.

Things I Wish I Knew Before Coming to Pitt

- It's a big party school.
- It's got a small campus feel.
- The city of Pittsburgh is actually very small.
- It's the perfect school for those with an undecided major.
- There are over 300 student organizations, including intramural sports.
- Sometimes you don't see the sunshine for days at a time.
- It's really easy to meet people on campus.
- If you move off campus, you can still get free access to Pitt Internet, even though it's just dial-up.

Tips to Succeed at Pitt

- Stick with classes you're interested in.
- Ask upperclassmen about classes or professors you're thinking about taking—they are one of the best resources for steering you in the right direction.
- Work hard, but take time to relax.
- Be outgoing—there's a lot to get involved in.
- Ask questions in class.
- Seek out your professors and TAs during office hours.

Pitt Urban Legends

- The Chancellor's Suite, on the 12th floor of Bruce Hall, is haunted.
- *Playboy* ranked Pitt's Hillman Library as one of the top places in the country to meet someone of the opposite sex.

School Spirit

Pitt students are known for having lots of school spirit. Faces are painted blue and gold, cheers are shouted at major sporting events, and many games sell out. Pitt gear is abundant around campus, and you'll even spot students or alumni across the country because of clothing, bumper stickers, or other slogans. The Oakland Zoo follows the Pitt basketball team with more passion than an over-acted soap opera. School pride isn't a requirement for coming to Pitt, but it doesn't need to be—students develop it well enough on their own.

Traditions

Hating Penn State

There's been a longstanding rivalry between Pitt and Penn State, the other college football giant of Pennsylvania. Anti-PSU shirts are sold on the streets in Oakland, and anyone who compares the Pitt Panther to a Nittany Lion is asking for trouble.

The Oakland Zoo

The official student section during basketball games; this is the place to be if you're a rabid fan.

The Panther

The panther was officially adopted as a mascot in 1909 for a number of reasons. Among them: the panther wasn't being used as any other school's mascot; its gold color was closest to the University's gold; it was already known as a noble animal; and, of course, the name alliterated quite well.

Tailgating

Be sure to get there early—real tailgating can start early on football weekends, (7 a.m. for a noon game), and it often ends long after the game at local house parties or fraternities.

The University Seal

Pitt's seal is a variation of William Pitt's coat of arms. William Pitt was the first Earl of Chatham and served as the British Prime Minister in the 18th century. On the seal, the three dots are gold coins, which denote the Pitt family's participation in the Crusades; the castle wall signifies the new city; the blue of the checkerboard represents Pitt's status as an Earl; and the white stands for purity, innocence, and gentleness.

The Varsity Walk

Between the Cathedral and the Heinz Chapel, you'll find the sidewalk lined with names, beginning in 1950, and continuing every year. This is the Varsity Walk, a tribute to students who have moved through the University with outstanding athletic and academic achievements.

Finding a Job or Internship

The Lowdown On...
Finding a Job or Internship

Career Services
224 William Pitt Union
(412) 648-7130
careers@pitt.edu
www.placement.pitt.edu

Career Services is a useful office at Pitt that's too often overlooked by students. The University provides a number of resources for students to build resumes, learn interviewing skills, and seek out valuable jobs and internships. In addition, every student is assigned an academic advisor to help you pick classes; these advisors can also counsel you about career options and the college pathways that will be most useful to you.

Advice

Get in touch with Career Services early, and keep checking with them throughout your time at Pitt! You must register with the office in order to access some valuable services, such as PantherTRACS (Tools for Recruiting And Career Services). These are more than worth the trouble of completing an application, and it's not going to cost you a dime.

Firms that Most Frequently Hire Graduates

ABC Sports, Abercrombie and Fitch, Allegheny County Bureau of Corrections, Allegheny County Jail, Allegheny Juvenile Court, American Eagle, Children's Hospital of Pittsburgh, Clear Channel, Comcast, Deloitte & Touche, Deloitte Consulting, Ford Motor Company, Heinz North America, Hershey Medical Center, Mellon Financial Corp., Newell Rubbermaid, PNC Financial Services Group, Pricewaterhouse Coopers, Primerica Financial Services, Reed Smith LLP, RiteAid Pharmacy, Schlumberger, Sears, United States Steel, University of Pittsburgh, University of Virginia, UPMC Health System, U.S. Air Force, US Navy, US Airways, US State Department, VA Medical Center, Walgreens, Walt Disney World, West Penn Hospital, Western Michigan University, Western Psychiatric Institute & Clinic

Grads Who Enter the Job Market Within

6 Months: N/A
1 Year: 77%

Alumni

The Lowdown On...
Alumni

Web Site:
www.alumni.pitt.edu

Alumni Office:
140 Alumni Hall
4227 Fifth Ave.
Pittsburgh, PA 15260
(800) 258-PITT

Services Available:
Alumni Recruitment Team
Career Assistance
Transcript Services

Major Alumni Events:
Alumni Trips
Homecoming

Alumni Publications:
Alumni Connections
The *Pitt Advocate*

Did You Know?

Famous Pitt Alumni:

Mike Bilirakis – U.S. Congressman

Ben Cardin – U.S. Congressman

Michael Chabon – Pulitzer Prize-winning author

Mike Ditka – American football hall-of-famer

Tony Dorsett – American football hall-of-famer

Tom Feeney – U.S. Congressman

Freddie Fu – Expert in sport medicine

Orrin Hatch – U.S. Senator

Dan Marino – Hall-of-fame NFL quarterback

Andrew W. Mellon – Banker, philanthropist, US Secretary of Treasury, and founder of the Mellon Institute of Science

Jim Moran – U.S. Congressman

John Murtha – U.S. Congressman

Leo Robin – American composer and songwriter

Rick Santorum – U.S. Senator

Dick Thornburgh – U.S. Attorney General (law degree)

James Traficant – U.S. Congressman

Lap-Chee Tsui – Genetic scientist

Albert Wynn – U.S. Congressman

Student Organizations

For the most up-to-date list of Pitt's student organizations, visit: *www.sorc.pitt.edu/search/index.html.*

- African American Coalition for Advancement, Achievement, Success and Excellence (AACAASE)
- African American Community of Entrepreneurial Students (ACES)
- African Students Organization
- Agape Christian Ministry
- AIESEC
- Ambassadors For Christ
- America Reads Challenge Student Organization
- American Chemical Society
- American Red Cross Club
- American Society of Civil Engineers
- American Society of Highway Engineers
- American Society of Mechanical Engineers
- Amizade Service Organization
- Amnesty International (undergraduate)
- Anointed Mime Ministry
- Anointed Steps of Faith
- Arnold Air Society
- Asian Christian Fellowship
- Asian Student Alliance
- Association for Computing Machinery
- Athletic Training Students Association
- Bachelor of Arts in Social Work Club (BASW Club)
- Badminton Club – the Berdz
- Beautiful Choice

- Best Buddies
- Biology Club
- Biomedical Engineering Society
- Black Action Society
- Black Dance Workshop
- Blue and Gold Society
- Brazil Nuts Porteguese Club
- Bread for the World
- Business Student Council
- Campus Anti-War Network (CAN)
- Campus Crusade for Christ
- Campus Fools
- Caribbean & Latin American Student Association (CLASA)
- Chabad House
- Chess Club
- Chinese American Students Association
- Christian Business Network
- Christians On Campus
- Circle K International
- College Democrats
- College Republicans
- Collegiate YMCA
- Cornerstone Christian Fellowship
- Creation Station (UPTV)
- CrossSeekers/Baptist Campus Ministry
- Dance Ensemble
- Deaf Awareness Society
- *Deek Magazine*
- Delta Chi
- Delta Sigma Pi
- Dental Science Club
- Do No Harm
- East West Martial Arts Club
- Eleanora Dusa Society
- Emergency Medical Services
- Engineering Student Council
- Exercise Physiology Club (Exercise Science Club)
- Filipino Students Association
- Freedom Mentoring and Leadership Development Honor Society
- Future Educators of America
- Gaming Club
- Gay-Straight Alliance
- Geology Club
- German Language and Literature Club
- Global Health Interest Group
- Golden Eagle African Student League
- Golden Key International Honor Society
- Hamagshimin Israel (HI)
- Hand in Hand Festival
- He Shan Shen Black Mountain Spirit Martial Arts
- Health Information Management Student Association
- Heinz Chapel Choir
- Hellenic Students Association
- Hillel Jewish University Center
- Hindu Student Council
- Hooligan Soccer Club
- IAESTE (International Association for the Exchange of Student for Technical Experience)
- Ice Hockey Club (Men's)
- Indian Subcontinent Association
- Institute of Electrical and Electronic Engineers (IEEE)
- Interactive Music and Simulation Organization (IMSO)
- Interfraternity Council (IFC)

- International Socialist Organization
- International Student Fellowship
- Intramural Softball
- Iranian Student Cultural Association
- Italian Club
- Japanese Culture Appreciation Club
- Japanese Speaking Society
- Jewish Heritage Program (JHP)
- Jewish Women's Organization
- Judo Organization
- Korean Culture Association
- Kuntu Repertory Theatre
- Lady Ice Panthers – Ice Hockey
- Lady Panther Lacrosse Club
- Lambda Sigma Honor Society
- Latin American Student Advisory Committee
- Lutheran Student Fellowship
- Medieval Interest Club
- Men's Glee Club
- Mi Gente Latinos Unidos
- Model United Nations
- Mortar Board Senior Honor Society
- Mu Kappa Upsilon
- Muslim Student Association
- National Pan-Hellenic Council (NPHC)
- National Residence Hall Honorary
- National Society of Black Engineers
- National Society of Collegiate Scholars (NSCS)
- National Student Partnerships
- National Student Speech Language Hearing Association (NSSLHA)
- Native American Student Organization
- Neuroscience Club
- Newman Oratory Catholic Organization
- Nurses Christian Fellowship
- Nursing Student Association
- Oakland Zoo Club
- Olympic Taekwondo Club
- Open Circle
- Organization for Women in Science
- Orthodox Christian Fellowship
- Outdoors Club
- Pan-Hellenic Association Sororities
- Panther Amateur Radio Club
- Panther Book Club
- Panther Bowling Club
- Panther Dance Twirl Club
- Panther Equestrian Club
- Panther Field Hockey
- Panther Habitat for Humanity
- Panther Investment Club
- Panther Lacrosse
- Panther Mock Trial Team
- Panther Paintball Club
- Panther Pocket Billiards Club
- Panther Pride Club
- Panther Rugby Football Club
- Panther Sports Network
- Panther Tango Club
- Panther Water Polo Club
- Panther Women's Rugby Football Club (PWRFC)
- Panthers for American Values
- *Papercut* Literary Magazine
- Philosophy Club
- Pitt African Drum Ensemble
- Pitt French Club
- Pitt in Hollywood

- Pitt Pathfinders
- Pitt Pendulums
- Pitt Program Council
- Pitt Rowing Club (crew)
- Pittsburgh Cadet Group
- Pittsburgh Fencing Association
- Pittsburgh First-Year Students (Hillel)
- Pittsburgh Intercollegiate Snowboard Team (PIST)
- Pittsburgh Japanese Animation Club
- Pittsburgh Men's Intercollegiate Soccer Club
- Pittsburgh Men's Volleyball
- Pittsburgh Representation of the Information Science Majors (PRISM)
- Pittsburgh Standard
- Pittsburgh Students Active in Lutheran Ministry (PSALM)
- *Pittsburgh Undergraduate Review*
- Polish Student Alliance
- Pre-Law Society
- Pre-Medical Organization for Minority Students (POMS)
- Psi Chi
- Quechua Club
- Rainbow Alliance
- Random Acts of Kindness
- Rehabilitation Science Student Association
- Resident Student Association
- Rho Chi Honorary Pharmacy Society
- Roberto Clemente Minority Business Association (RCMBA)
- Robotics Club
- Russian Club
- Saudi Student Club
- Shoes That Fit
- Shotokan Karate Club
- Sigma Alpha Lambda
- Sigma Gamma Epsilon
- Sisters Beyond the Surface
- Ski & Snowboard Club
- Society for Creative Interactive Theater
- Society for International Business
- Society of Automotive Engineers (SAE)
- Some of God's Children Gospel Choir
- Sounds Of Pleasure
- Spanish Club
- Spiritist Studies Group
- STAY Pittsburgh (Students for a Younger Pittsburgh)
- Steadfast Anchors Club
- Steel City Underground Theatre Society
- Student Citizenship Alliance
- Student Community Organizing Project
- Student Dietetic Association of the School of Health and Rehabilitation Sciences
- Student Entrepreneurship Administration
- Student Global AIDS Project
- Student Government Board (SGB)
- Student Slovak Club
- Students and Latinos United Against Disparities (SALUD)
- Students for a Sensible Drug Policy
- Students for Justice in Palestine
- Students for Political Opportunity
- Students in Solidarity
- Students of the Department of

Africana Studies
Students Seeking a Cure
Table Tennis Club
Tau Beta Pi
Tau Beta Sigma
Tennis Club
The ASM – TMS Joint Student Chapter (Materials)
The Child Development Association
The Cotton Club
The Film Club
The New Fangled Old Tyme Vaudeville Company
The Sprocket Guild
The Writer's Bloc
Theta Nu Xi Multicultural Sorority, Inc.
Turkish American Student Association
Tzu-Ching Student Organization (TCSO)
Ukrainian Student Organization
Ultimate Frisbee Club
Undergraduate ACLU Club
Undergraduate Anthropology Club
Undergraduate Communication Club
Undergraduate Economics Society
Undergraduate Finance Club
Undergraduate Marketing Club
United Interfellowship
United Parker's Kenpo Club
University Chinese Club of Pittsburgh
University Handbell Ensemble
University of Pittsburgh Chapter of SIAM
Urban Studies Association
Vietnamese Student Association
Voices for Animal Liberation
Women's Chorale Ensemble
Women's Ultimate Frisbee
Women's Volleyball Club
WPTS-FM
Yinzer Association of Pittsburgh: Yinzling

The Best & Worst

The Ten **BEST** Things About Pitt

1. $1 movies in the Union
2. SafeRider, for getting home after late-night parties
3. "History of Jazz" with Nathan Davis
4. Dave and Andy's ice cream
5. Buses home for holidays
6. Peter's Pub on Thursday nights
7. Nationally-ranked football and basketball teams
8. Tailgating
9. Friday Night Improvs
10. Oakland restaurants and bars

The Ten WORST Things About Pitt

1. Foreign teaching assistants
2. Parking (or lack thereof)
3. Hiking up "Cardiac Hill"
4. Waiting for shuttles and buses
5. On-campus meals
6. Large introductory lectures
7. Fighting to get basketball tickets
8. Winter weather
9. Campus building security
10. South Oakland on weekends

Visiting

The Lowdown On...
Visiting

Hotel Information:

Best Western University Center
3401 Boulevard of the Allies, Oakland
(412) 683-6100
(800) 245-4444
www.bestwestern.com
Distance from Campus: Less than a mile
Price Range: $85–$99

Hampton Inn
3315 Hamlet Street, Oakland
(412) 681-1000
(800) HAMPTON
www.pittsburghhamptoninn.com
Distance from Campus: Less than a mile
Price Range: $89–$119

Hilton Towers
600 Commonwealth Pl.,
Downtown
(412) 391-4600
www.hilton.com
Distance from Campus:
3.4 miles
Price Range: $190–$250

Holiday Inn Select – University Center
100 Lytton Ave., Oakland
(412) 682-6200
(800) 864-8287
www.holiday-inn.com
Distance from Campus:
Less than a mile
Price Range: $123–$144

Residence Inn by Marriott
3896 Bigelow Blvd., Oakland
(412) 621-2200
(800) 331-3131
www.residenceinn.com
Distance from Campus:
Less than a mile
Price Range: $139–$189

University Club
123 University Pl., Oakland
(412) 621-1890
Distance from Campus:
Less than a mile
Price Range: $99–$109

Wyndham Garden Hotel – University Place
3454 Forbes Ave., Oakland
(412) 683-2040
www.wyndham.com
Distance from Campus:
Less than a mile
Price Range: $89–$129

Shadyside Inn
5405 Fifth Ave., Shadyside
(412) 682-2300
www.shadysideinn.com
Distance from Campus:
1.4 miles
Price Range: $99–$150

Sunnyledge
5124 Fifth Ave., Shadyside
(412) 683-5014
www.sunnyledge.com
Distance from Campus:
1.1 miles
Price Range: $189–$275

Omni William Penn
530 William Penn Pl.,
Downtown
(412) 281-7100
www.omnihotels.com
Distance from Campus:
3.3 miles
Price Range: $116–$159

Take a Campus Virtual Tour

www.umc.pitt.edu/tour

To Schedule a Group Information Session or Interview

Information sessions are generally held on select Saturday mornings at 9 a.m. Schedule online at www.pitt.edu/~oafa/visit.html, or call the admissions office at (412) 624-7488.

Campus Tours

Campus tours are given Monday through Friday at 10 a.m., 11 a.m., 1 p.m., 2 p.m., and 3 p.m. Tours are not given on holidays or between semesters. Call (412) 624-7717 for specific details.

Overnight Visits

Call the admissions office to set up overnights at (412) 624-7488.

Directions to Campus

Driving from the North/West

- Take the Pennsylvania Turnpike east to Exit 28, Perry Highway.
- Follow Interstate 79 South to 279 South (Exit 72).
- Follow signs and go over the Fort Duquesne Bridge.
- Take 376 East to Exit 2A, Forbes Avenue/Oakland.
- Stay in the left-hand lane, following Forbes until you get to Bigelow Boulevard.
- Make a left onto Bigelow Boulevard.
- Go straight through the first light across Fifth Avenue, and make a left into the Soldiers and Sailors parking garage.

Driving from the South

- Take Interstate 79 North to 279 North (Pittsburgh).
- Follow 279 North toward Pittsburgh through the Fort Pitt Tunnel and onto the Fort Pitt Bridge.
- Once on the bridge, stay in the far right lanes and follow signs for 376 East/Monroeville.
- Take 376 East to Exit 2A, Forbes Avenue/Oakland.
- Stay in the left-hand lane, following Forbes until you get to Bigelow Boulevard.
- Make a left onto Bigelow Boulevard.
- Go straight through the first light across Fifth Avenue, and make a left into the Soldiers and Sailors parking garage.

Driving from the East

- Take the Pennsylvania Turnpike West to Exit 57, Pittsburgh/Monroeville.
- Follow Interstate 376 West to Exit 3A, Oakland.
- Keep right at the end of the ramp, and stay in the right-hand lane.
- Go straight through the first light across the Boulevard of the Allies (at the top of the hill), go straight through the light at Atwood Street, and follow the road (Bates Street) until it ends on South Bouquet Street.
- Make a left on South Bouquet Street and follow it until the first light at Forbes Avenue.
- Make a right onto Forbes Avenue, staying in the left-hand lane, following Forbes until you get to Bigelow Boulevard.
- Make a left onto Bigelow Boulevard.
- Go straight through the first light across Fifth Avenue, and make a left into the Soldiers and Sailors parking garage.

Words to Know

Academic Probation – A suspension imposed on a student if he or she fails to keep up with the school's minimum academic requirements. Those unable to improve their grades after receiving this warning can face dismissal.

Beer Pong/Beirut – A drinking game involving cups of beer arranged in a pyramid shape on each side of a table. The goal is to get a ping pong ball into one of the opponent's cups by throwing the ball or hitting it with a paddle. If the ball lands in a cup, the opponent is required to drink the beer.

Bid – An invitation from a fraternity or sorority to 'pledge' (join) that specific house.

Blue-Light Phone – Brightly-colored phone posts with a blue light bulb on top. These phones exist for security purposes and are located at various outside locations around most campuses. In an emergency, a student can pick up one of these phones (free of charge) to connect with campus police or a security escort.

Campus Police – Police who are specifically assigned to a given institution. Campus police are typically not regular city officers; they are employed by the university in a full-time capacity.

Club Sports – A level of sports that falls somewhere between varsity and intramural. If a student is unable to commit to a varsity team but has a lot of passion for athletics, a club sport could be a better, less intense option. Even less demanding, intramural (IM) sports often involve no traveling and considerably less time.

Cocaine – An illegal drug. Also known as "coke" or "blow," cocaine often resembles a white crystalline or powdery substance. It is highly addictive and dangerous.

Common Application – An application with which students can apply to multiple schools.

Course Registration – The period of official class selection for the upcoming quarter or semester. Prior to registration, it is best to prepare several back-up courses in case a particular class becomes full. If a course is full, students can place themselves on the waitlist, although this still does not guarantee entry.

Division Athletics – Athletic classifications range from Division I to Division III. Division IA is the most competitive, while Division III is considered to be the least competitive.

Dorm – A dorm (or dormitory) is an on-campus housing facility. Dorms can provide a range of options from suite-style rooms to more communal options that include shared bathrooms. Most first-year students live in dorms. Some upperclassmen who wish to stay on campus also choose this option.

Early Action – An application option with which a student can apply to a school and receive an early acceptance response without a binding commitment. This system is becoming less and less available.

Early Decision – An application option that students should use only if they are certain they plan to attend the school in question. If a student applies using the early decision option and is admitted, he or she is required and bound to attend that university. Admission rates are usually higher among students who apply through early decision, as the student is clearly indicating that the school is his or her first choice.

Ecstasy – An illegal drug. Also known as "E" or "X," ecstasy looks like a pill and most resembles an aspirin. Considered a party drug, ecstasy is very dangerous and can be deadly.

Ethernet – An extremely fast Internet connection available in most university-owned residence halls. To use an Ethernet connection properly, a student will need a network card and cable for his or her computer.

Fake ID – A counterfeit identification card that contains false information. Most commonly, students get fake IDs with altered birthdates so that they appear to be older than 21 (and therefore of legal drinking age). Even though it is illegal, many college students have fake IDs in hopes of purchasing alcohol or getting into bars.

Frosh – Slang for "freshman" or "freshmen."

Hazing – Initiation rituals administered by some fraternities or sororities as part of the pledging process. Many universities have outlawed hazing due to its degrading, and sometimes dangerous, nature.

Intramurals (IMs) – A popular, and usually free, sport league in which students create teams and compete against one another. These sports vary in competitiveness and can include a range of activities—everything from billiards to water polo. IM sports are a great way to meet people with similar interests.

Keg – Officially called a half-barrel, a keg contains roughly 200 12-ounce servings of beer.

LSD – An illegal drug, also known as acid, this hallucinogenic drug most commonly resembles a tab of paper.

Marijuana – An illegal drug, also known as weed or pot; along with alcohol, marijuana is one of the most commonly-found drugs on campuses across the country.

Major –The focal point of a student's college studies; a specific topic that is studied for a degree. Examples of majors include physics, English, history, computer science, economics, business, and music. Many students decide on a specific major before arriving on campus, while others are simply "undecided" until declaring a major. Those who are extremely interested in two areas can also choose to double major.

Meal Block – The equivalent of one meal. Students on a meal plan usually receive a fixed number of meals per week. Each meal, or "block," can be redeemed at the school's dining facilities in place of cash. Often, a student's weekly allotment of meal blocks will be forfeited if not used.

Minor – An additional focal point in a student's education. Often serving as a complement or addition to a student's main area of focus, a minor has fewer requirements and prerequisites to fulfill than a major. Minors are not required for graduation from most schools; however some students who want to explore many different interests choose to pursue both a major and a minor.

Mushrooms – An illegal drug. Also known as "'shrooms," this drug resembles regular mushrooms but is extremely hallucinogenic.

Off-Campus Housing – Housing from a particular landlord or rental group that is not affiliated with the university. Depending on the college, off-campus housing can range from extremely popular to non-existent. Students who choose to live off campus are typically given more freedom, but they also have to deal with possible subletting scenarios, furniture, bills, and other issues. In addition to these factors, rental prices and distance often affect a student's decision to move off campus.

Office Hours – Time that teachers set aside for students who have questions about coursework. Office hours are a good forum for students to go over any problems and to show interest in the subject material.

Pledging – The early phase of joining a fraternity or sorority, pledging takes place after a student has gone through rush and received a bid. Pledging usually lasts between one and two semesters. Once the pledging period is complete and a particular student has done everything that is required to become a member, that student is considered a brother or sister. If a fraternity or a sorority would decide to "haze" a group of students, this initiation would take place during the pledging period.

Private Institution – A school that does not use tax revenue to subsidize education costs. Private schools typically cost more than public schools and are usually smaller.

Prof – Slang for "professor."

Public Institution – A school that uses tax revenue to subsidize education costs. Public schools are often a good value for in-state residents and tend to be larger than most private colleges.

Quarter System (or Trimester System) – A type of academic calendar system. In this setup, students take classes for three academic periods. The first quarter usually starts in late September or early October and concludes right before Christmas. The second quarter usually starts around early to mid-January and finishes up around March or April. The last academic quarter, or "third quarter," usually starts in late March or early April and finishes up in late May or Mid-June. The fourth quarter is summer. The major difference between the quarter system and semester system is that students take more, less comprehensive courses under the quarter calendar.

RA (Resident Assistant) – A student leader who is assigned to a particular floor in a dormitory in order to help to the other students who live there. An RA's duties include ensuring student safety and providing assistance wherever possible.

Recitation – An extension of a specific course; a review session. Some classes, particularly large lectures, are supplemented with mandatory recitation sessions that provide a relatively personal class setting.

Rolling Admissions – A form of admissions. Most commonly found at public institutions, schools with this type of policy continue to accept students throughout the year until their class sizes are met. For example, some schools begin accepting students as early as December and will continue to do so until April or May.

Room and Board – This figure is typically the combined cost of a university-owned room and a meal plan.

Room Draw/Housing Lottery – A common way to pick on-campus room assignments for the following year. If a student decides to remain in university-owned housing, he or she is assigned a unique number that, along with seniority, is used to determine his or her housing for the next year.

Rush – The period in which students can meet the brothers and sisters of a particular chapter and find out if a given fraternity or sorority is right for them. Rushing a fraternity or a sorority is not a requirement at any school. The goal of rush is to give students who are serious about pledging a feel for what to expect.

Semester System – The most common type of academic calendar system at college campuses. This setup typically includes two semesters in a given school year. The fall semester starts around the end of August or early September and concludes before winter vacation. The spring semester usually starts in mid-January and ends in late April or May.

Student Center/Rec Center/Student Union – A common area on campus that often contains study areas, recreation facilities, and eateries. This building is often a good place to meet up with fellow students; depending on the school, the student center can have a huge role or a non-existent role in campus life.

Student ID – A university-issued photo ID that serves as a student's key to school-related functions. Some schools require students to show these cards in order to get into dorms, libraries, cafeterias, and other facilities. In addition to storing meal plan information, in some cases, a student ID can actually work as a debit card and allow students to purchase things from bookstores or local shops.

Suite – A type of dorm room. Unlike dorms that feature communal bathrooms shared by the entire floor, suites offer bathrooms shared only among the suite. Suite-style dorm rooms can house anywhere from two to ten students.

TA (Teacher's Assistant) – An undergraduate or grad student who helps in some manner with a specific course. In some cases, a TA will teach a class, assist a professor, grade assignments, or conduct office hours.

Undergraduate – A student in the process of studying for his or her bachelor's degree.

ABOUT THE AUTHORS

Writing this book was quite an experience! I came to College Prowler over a year ago, just going into my senior year, and got to experience the blooming of the company almost right from the start. Now that I'm a "super senior"—a.k.a. a fifth year senior soon to graduate—I am so blessed to have had the opportunity to write for such a great company. This book was tons of fun to write, and I hope that you enjoy reading it as much as I enjoyed writing it. If this book helps you in the least, even if you decide that Pitt isn't for you, then I have done my job as a writer in conveying information to help you make an educated decision about college. I believe that college is the best four (or five or six) years of your life, and hopefully our guidebooks help you to gather enough information to ensure that you feel the same way when your college graduation creeps up on you!

I would just like to say thank you to the staff at College Prowler for giving me the opportunity to write for a company that I am proud to belong to. For all your support, encouragement, and faith in me, I cannot say thank you enough.

Jamie Cruttenden
jamiecruttenden@collegeprowler.com

ABOUT THE AUTHORS

Though I'm originally from Penn State's backyard, I've called Pittsburgh home since my freshman year of college. For most of that time, I've been working with College Prowler in some capacity and couldn't be more thrilled to co-author the book for my own school. There's so much to do in Pittsburgh that I didn't discover until my second semester, or later, and after only my first year, I realize how important it is to have a definitive campus guide. Don't stop here, though—if you're moving to Pittsburgh, it's a great idea to check online and watch publications such as the *City Paper* for cultural events and community happenings. There's a lot more going on than you'd expect at first glance.

When I'm not helping out with the guidebook series, I can be found at Pitt as a poetry writing major, in city parks sitting under trees, or around Squirrel Hill as a general miscreant. If you liked this book, be sure to check out the PSU guide—just don't tell anyone I recommended it!

Tim Williams
timwilliams@collegeprowler.com

Notes

Notes

Notes

California Colleges

**California dreamin'?
This book is a must have for you!**

CALIFORNIA COLLEGES
7¼" X 10", 762 Pages Paperback
$29.95 Retail
1-59658-501-3

Stanford, UC Berkeley, Caltech—California is home to some of America's greatest institutes of higher learning. *California Colleges* gives the lowdown on 24 of the best, side by side, in one prodigious volume.

New England Colleges

**Looking for peace in the Northeast?
Pick up this regional guide to New England!**

NEW ENGLAND COLLEGES
7¼" X 10", 1015 Pages Paperback
$29.95 Retail
1-59658-504-8

New England is the birthplace of many prestigious universities, and with so many to choose from, picking the right school can be a tough decision. With inside information on over 34 competive Northeastern schools, *New England Colleges* provides the same high-quality information prospective students expect from College Prowler in one all-inclusive, easy-to-use reference.

Schools of the South

Headin' down south? This book will help you find your way to the perfect school!

SCHOOLS OF THE SOUTH
7¼" X 10", 773 Pages Paperback
$29.95 Retail
1-59658-503-X

Southern pride is always strong. Whether it's across town or across state, many Southern students are devoted to their home sweet home. *Schools of the South* offers an honest student perspective on 36 universities available south of the Mason-Dixon.

Untangling the Ivy League

The ultimate book for everything Ivy!

UNTANGLING THE IVY LEAGUE
7¼" X 10", 567 Pages Paperback
$24.95 Retail
1-59658-500-5

Ivy League students, alumni, admissions officers, and other top insiders get together to tell it like it is. *Untangling the Ivy League* covers every aspect—from admissions and athletics to secret societies and urban legends—of the nation's eight oldest, wealthiest, and most competitive colleges and universities.

Need Help Paying For School?

Apply for our scholarship!

College Prowler awards thousands of dollars a year to students who compose the best essays. E-mail scholarship@collegeprowler.com for more information, or call 1-800-290-2682.

Apply now at **www.collegeprowler.com**

COLLEGE PROWLER®

Tell Us What Life Is Really Like at Your School!

Have you ever wanted to let people know what your college is really like? Now's your chance to help millions of high school students choose the right college.

Let your voice be heard.

Check out **www.collegeprowler.com** for more info!

College Prowler®

Need More Help?

Do you have more questions about this school? Can't find a certain statistic? College Prowler is here to help. We are the best source of college information out there. We have a network of thousands of students who can get the latest information on any school to you ASAP. E-mail us at info@collegeprowler.com with your college-related questions.

E-Mail Us Your College-Related Questions!

Check out *www.collegeprowler.com* for more details.
1-800-290-2682

COLLEGE PROWLER®

Write For Us!
Get published! Voice your opinion.

Writing a College Prowler guidebook is both fun and rewarding; our open-ended format allows your own creativity free reign. Our writers have been featured in national newspapers and have seen their names in bookstores across the country. Now is your chance to break into the publishing industry with one of the country's fastest-growing publishers!

Apply now at **www.collegeprowler.com**

Contact editor@collegeprowler.com or call 1-800-290-2682 for more details.

COLLEGE PROWLER®

Pros and Cons

Still can't figure out if this is the right school for you? You've already read through this in-depth guide; why not list the pros and cons? It will really help with narrowing down your decision and determining whether or not this school is right for you.

Pros	Cons
....	....
....	....
....	....
....	....
....	....
....	....
....	....
....	....
....	....
....	....
....	....
....	....
....	....

COLLEGE PROWLER®

Pros and Cons

Still can't figure out if this is the right school for you? You've already read through this in-depth guide; why not list the pros and cons? It will really help with narrowing down your decision and determining whether or not this school is right for you.

Pros	**Cons**
....	....
....	....
....	....
....	....
....	....
....	....
....	....
....	....
....	....
....	....
....	....
....	....
....	....
....	....

Notes

Notes